How, Why, and When We Eat Flowers

Edible Flowers

Monica Nelson

Photographs by Adrianna Glaviano

Contents

I once watched an iguana weave his way through a garden of ferns.
He would lift his head to casually bite off a papery purple flower, carry
on, then bite off another. My initial response was to judge the behavior
insolent, but I softened as I watched half a dozen flowers disappear from
the landscaping, gradually understanding the impulse. It's the same
impulse I see in photos my friend sends me of her five-year-old daughter, her pockets stuffed full of flowers she's collected on walks. Or, as
Robin Wall Kimmerer writes in *Braiding Sweetgrass*, "How do I show my
girls I love them?... In May we pick violets and go swimming in July."

We live with flowers, and sometimes for them. Flowers have been
folded into our lives for centuries. Petals were strewn across medieval
meals and said to have tinted the water that Cleopatra bathed in. Flowers
set sail in some of the earliest ships of trade, and those that remained
rooted in gardens provided places of refuge. Flowers have often been the
dedicated catalysts for artistic creation, and have given women an entrée
into science. Sometimes they did both—as evidenced by Emily Dickinson's
Herbarium, a meticulously organized catalogue of some four hundred
flowers she collected and studied. Despite how closely they have been
classified and organized, how extensively they have been cultivated, and
valued, and traded, how much art and literature they have inspired,
a sense of impulse guides all of our interactions with flowers.

A blossom marks time keenly and suddenly; as in spring, when
you look up to discover the world has effloresced. There is a proprietary
sense felt toward flowers, as if a bloom—even in a public garden—were
only for you. A moment staring at a flower is full of love, presence, and
discovery: an entire tiny universe in front of you, ripe for the taking as
both a metaphor and an offering. The impulse to stuff flowers into your
pockets is perhaps more natural than to create an elaborate arrangement
with them, the urge to eat them truer than to watch them wilt slowly. To
casually bite into a blossom before it falls off with time.

Flowers exist by attracting attention; they rely on impulse. The biology of a flower allows it varying degrees of self-sufficiency, and considering that the blossom is a plant's reproductive organ, its visceral quality is no mistake; it wants to be noticed. The brightly colored and textured petals have evolved over time with the specific purpose of consummation, and their role in the ecosystem relies on them being beheld, pollinated, and utilized. Flowers produce food in the form of nectar, pollen, and oils that attract bees, butterflies, and birds and keep the environment around them healthy. That flowers can be picked, pickled, baked, and candied adds an extra phase to the life cycle of a flower—a phase this book illuminates by highlighting the uses of flowers in contemporary and historical culinary practices and investigating how the impulse to share, eat, and distribute flowers has been integral to our cultures.

Claudia Roden, the Egyptian-born food writer and historian who often writes of flower-infused recipes from the past, told the *New Yorker* in 2007 that while cooking medieval dishes and food related to her heritage, she was overcome by history and "the idea that through food you could describe or reconstruct a world." Edible flowers provide a similarly rich lens through which to see. You learn quickly that rose (p. 193) and orange blossoms (p. 71) have been distilled for centuries in the Middle East to flavor sweets and coffee. The Aztecs used marigolds (p. 144) to flavor cacao. Daylily (p. 94) is an important element in Chinese cooking. Some flowers are older than recorded history, yet remain widespread—even too widespread, in the case of invasive species—like wood sorrel (p. 214), which can be seen in Renaissance paintings as well as crowding around playground swing sets. Or dandelion (p. 93), a bitter herb of the Bible that has persisted through time and is hardy enough still to grow through concrete sidewalks.

The practice of eating flowers has ebbed and flowed with the tides of culinary custom, but is today a growing force among restaurants that incorporate seasonal farming into their menus. Most notably, Chez Panisse, in Berkeley, California, has grown an edible flower garden since it opened in 1971. René Redzepi, the chef and co-owner of the Scandinavian restaurant Noma, uses edible flowers in over ninety of the recipes in his book *Noma: Time and Place in Nordic Cuisine*, and flowers are on frequent rotation in dishes at the restaurant. Quintonil, in Mexico City, features edible flowers in many of its dishes, including a tiny quail engulfed in lilac (p. 136), nasturtium (p. 159), cockscomb (p. 72), marigold, and waxy green leaves, which gives the poetic appearance of an animal protein being summoned back into nature.

There is an allure to eating flowers, one that harks back to this feeling of impulse and the desire to consume a whole, beautiful thing. A flower is the seed-bearing part of a plant that includes the pollen-coated stamens (the "male" parts) and the pistils (the "female" parts). These are surrounded by petals that vary in size, shape, and color and bloom from the calyx, which protects the flower as a bud and then supports it once it blossoms. Edible flowers, which serve the same ecological function as all flowers—to spread and propagate—have a varied life as food. For example, broccoli, cauliflower, artichoke (p. 27), and brussels sprouts are so commonplace that they are rarely thought of as flowering plants. To an eater, the blossoming of an herb such as basil (p. 31) marks the end of its sweetest phase, while the flowering of okra (p. 164) marks the beginning: it blooms briefly, its white flower like a soft alarm signaling the bud of its fruit.

This book highlights more than one hundred flowers that are largely present in North America and Europe, though the overall scope is wider. The research is presented in a concise portrait of each flower that focuses on its appearance, cultural history, and how it may be eaten. We have employed the most common English names for the basis of our alphabetization, but Latin genus names such as *Allium* (p. 108) speak to a larger group. Notes for each flower provide its blooming season, place of origin, and plant type—either a flowering tree, shrub, vine, or forb. But the purpose of this book is to serve as an inspiring primer, not a definitive guide to the horticulture of edible flowers. My hope is that this book will spark curiosity and set readers off in a number of directions.

In photographing the flowers and designing this book, it was important to foster a sense of immersion. In some instances, the flowers were simply laid on a scanner; these intimate images place the flower as close as possible to its viewer, as if it's ready to be picked back up at any moment. But the majority of the photos are by Adrianna Glaviano, a photographer whose sensibility is visceral and impulsive. Her images capture each flower in its own divine light, often in its natural growing state. In other photos, we pressed the flower between glass and held it to the sky. These images evoke the formality of botanical drawings while maintaining the flower's natural imperfections. When photographing food, accessibility was at the forefront. Flowers are precious, beautiful things; but in this world, you live with them. The design of the book is also immersive. The imagery is separated from its description, like plates in a reference book, and the small size of the book keeps reading comfortable, allowing the book itself to also be lived with.

At one of the first farms Adrianna and I visited, the owner casually plucked the blossom of a cornflower (p. 85) off its stem and popped it into his mouth. We also snacked on tiny gem marigolds that expanded with a citrus flavor as we chewed. These plants were grown pesticide-free, of course, and this is one of the most important things to note when consuming flowers. As important as terroir is to viticulture, where a flower grows, and how, determines its edibility beyond its inherent nontoxicity (please note the list of common toxic flowers on page 17).

But even grown under perfect conditions, there is an uneasy feeling when watching someone bite the head off a rose, and perhaps a bit of that feeling also permeates this book. "Rewilding" is an idea that is being incorporated into culture at scale; native plants are being returned to the land where they originated, enticing pollinators, and so forth. Perhaps with each bite, a little rewilding can happen within everyone.

Years ago, a friend brought a handful of buzz buttons (p. 51) to my apartment to share with a small group of friends. We sat together letting the flowers fizz on our tongues. Much has been said poetically about flowers, but the experience of eating them remains with you.

You always remember eating a flower.

Edible Flowers

Daisy fleabane

Introduction

Rose

Edible Flowers

How to Eat Flowers

This book profiles more than one hundred flowers that are edible, which is defined as nontoxic and safe for human consumption. However, as with all things, moderation is key: while some flowers may be perfectly edible in small quantities, consuming too many can lead to adverse reactions. Another very important thing to consider is seasonal allergies, as all flowers contain pollen.

One rule of thumb when served a flower at a restaurant is that if it's on a plate, it's edible. Otherwise, even when purchasing the flower directly from a farm, there are many factors that can compromise its edibility, including the soil in which it was grown and the treatment it received. It's difficult to ascertain the growing conditions of chamomile and tulips, for example, when purchased at a grocery store or bodega, or even certain nurseries.

Similarly, if you find Queen Anne's lace, elderflower, or chicory on the side of the road, clip mindfully. If the road is heavily trafficked, the flowers may have absorbed toxins from car fumes, or waste from animals. Sourcing organically grown flowers meant for consumption is always best.

If you grow edible flowers, collect them from your garden in the morning or in cooler temperatures, then wash them thoroughly in ice water to dislodge any dirt or bugs, and refrigerate them. Before eating flowers, remove the pistils and stamens. It's always best to eat the petals; some plants may have edible flowers, but toxic leaves or seeds.

Flowers are best eaten within a few days of collecting them, and never eat them if mold has grown on them. If you plan to dry the flowers, gather them later in the afternoon, when there is no dew, and then prepare them for drying by hanging or laying them out on a screen in a warm, dry place.

Finally, any harvesting of edible flowers in the wild should be done with an abundance of caution or, even better, the guidance of a knowledgeable forager or horticulturist. Many flowers look similar and it can sometimes be difficult to distinguish an edible flower from its toxic cousin.

Do not eat these common flowers:

Anemone	Milkweed
Azalea	Morning glory
Buttercup	Nightshades, such
Calla lily	as eggplant
Clematis	Oleander
Daffodil	Rhododendron
Delphinium	Spring Adonis
Hyacinth	Spurge
Hydrangea	Sweet pea
Iris	Trumpet flower
Lantana	Wisteria
Lily of the valley	
Lobelia	

Edible Flowers

Flowers

Artichoke

Buckwheat

Angelonia

Acacia

24

Acacia

The flowers of *Acacia dealbata*, also known as mimosa and silver wattle, are small, fuzzy yellow puffs that are edible, though full of pollen. President Thomas Jefferson, whose heirloom varieties of acacia still grow at the site of his plantation, Monticello, described acacia as "the most delicious flowering shrub in the world," adding that it was "the only plant besides the orange that I would take the trouble of nursing in a greenhouse." When harvesting acacia, take care to pluck or procure the flowers of *Acacia dealbata* in particular. Some other species of acacia are poisonous.

Image – p. 24

Alyssum

Alyssum is a low-growing flowering plant that can be found creeping along stone walls in Mediterranean landscapes, which its specific epithet, *maritima*, suggests. It blooms in small, round clusters of tiny, white, four-petaled flowers. The flowers bloom throughout the year in temperate coastal climates, and, in some cultivars, also appear in pale yellows, pinks, and purples. The plant is a member of the Brassicaceae family, which includes kale, cauliflower, and broccoli, and alyssum has a similarly sweet and peppery flavor. Both the stems and flowers can be added to soups, desserts, and salads, or used to garnish main courses.

Angelonia angustifolia

Angelonia

Origin Mexico, South America
Type Forb
Blooms Summer

Flowers of the genus *Angelonia* resemble miniature snapdragons (p. 200), but while the snapdragon has several hinged petals, angelonia has a single fused petal. The flower, which comes in white or vibrant shades of blue and purple, originated in Mexico and South America, and only recently, in the past fifty years, has it been integrated widely into gardens worldwide. Angelonia can be added to dishes as a garnish or used to decorate cakes.

Image – p. 21

Malus domestica

Apple Blossom

Origin Europe
Type Flowering tree
Blooms Spring

One of the most sweetly regarded and fragrant flowers is the apple blossom. It is hard to have anything but charming associations with the small pink petals that dust otherwise green apple orchards at the first hint of spring. The delicate white and pink blossoms are a welcome sign of the changing seasons and fill the air with a strong honeysuckle scent that attracts their chief pollinators, bees. In 1897 the apple blossom was designated the official flower of Michigan, though the state is today third in the country in apple production, just behind Washington and New York. When eaten, apple blossoms have a perfumed, floral flavor. They are a nice accompaniment to many desserts, and can be added to fruit salads, or candied to use as a delicate garnish on cakes and tarts.

Image – p. 22

Cynara cardunculus

Artichoke

Origin Mediterranean
Type Forb
Blooms Summer

The artichoke resembles a prehistoric visitor with its cartoonishly oversized scales and bulbous shape. Its large, leathery head jutting from a patch of otherwise delicate plants gives it the look of a dinosaur. The artichoke has grown wild across the Mediterranean basin since at least 300 BCE, when the Greek philosopher and naturalist Theophrastus first wrote of it. The hardy plant was later called one of "the monstrosities of the Earth" by Pliny the Elder in his *Natural History* of 77 CE, although he also generously noted its "pleasant flavor."

The artichoke's culinary history has taken many twists and turns as it bobbed in and out of favor. Wealthy Romans enjoyed artichokes preserved in honey cut with vinegar and seasoned with cumin (or the mysterious herb silphium, which was so prized by ancient gourmands, it is thought to have been overharvested to extinction). For centuries after the fall of Rome, the plant was mostly cultivated in the Arab world, with growing resuming in Europe in the 1500s. In 1787, while traveling through Italy, the German writer, poet, and playwright Johann Wolfgang von Goethe wrote of observing, with amazement, two Sicilian noblemen cut artichokes from their stems, peel their barbed outer petals, and devour the hearts. Soon after, in 1806, French immigrants settling in the Louisiana Territory brought artichokes to the United States. By the early 1900s, the American artichoke market was controlled by the Mafia, who threatened and extorted artichoke farmers. These so-called artichoke wars lasted years and led New York Mayor Fiorello La Guardia to prohibit the "sale, display, and possession of artichokes" in 1935.

The globe-shaped artichoke best known today is thought to be a domesticated variety of the more ancient cardoon, which had a slightly pricklier and pinker head. The artichoke head is itself the bud of the plant, and it is most edible right before it opens into the stringy, bright purple flowering orb. The whole of the artichoke head is edible, and

(cont.)

(Artichoke, cont.)

the scalelike bracts have been present in cuisines for centuries. To eat an artichoke, though, takes time. It requires softening the meat of the bracts and heart, often by steaming or roasting with an abundance of olive oil. The artichoke's nutty flavor pairs well with herbs such as parsley or thyme, and it is often accompanied by aioli or stuffed with breadcrumbs and cheese.

Image – p. 19

Eruca vesicaria

Arugula

Origin Mediterranean
Type Forb
Blooms Spring, fall

As Iowa arugula grower Carl Glanzman noted during an interview for PBS, "[Arugula] thrives well on total abuse." Which may be why this leafy, peppery flowering green has flourished for millennia. Arugula can grow in most places and alongside most other plants; in grass, among weeds, even in cold weather, it persists. However, despite how commonplace it may be in the United States today—it's often found strewn across pizzas, heaped as beds for braised fish, or prewashed and packaged in plastic clamshells at your local supermarket—arugula has only been popular in America for around twenty years. In that short time, and in line with its hardy nature and piquant character, it has managed to attract controversy. In 2007, it was characterized by some as being elite when President Barack Obama remarked on the high price of arugula during a campaign speech. Arugula was soon sidelined by kale, but remains a sturdy, spicy standby.

Arugula, called rocket in the United Kingdom, is mentioned in the Old Testament and was famously extolled as an aphrodisiac by the Roman poets Virgil and Ovid. It was because of this reputation that the Roman Catholic Church forbade the growing of arugula in its monastery gardens.

Native to the Mediterranean, arugula has been present in the cuisines of this region for centuries. Both the leaves and blossoms

(Arugula, cont.)

are edible. The arugula flower—small, with four cream-colored petals each with a purple line down its center—tastes peppery, verdant, and a bit nutty. Arugula blossom seeds are cold-pressed to produce taramira oil, which can be applied topically to the skin and hair. In Asia the seeds are also used for pickling. In Egypt, fresh arugula flowers popularly accompany a breakfast of *ful medames*, stewed and spiced fava beans.

Image – p. 23

Aster spp.

Aster

Origin Europe
Type Forb
Blooms Late summer, fall

Flowers of the genus *Aster* are daisylike, often purple, and can commonly be found blanketing roadsides and fields as the summer heat begins to cool. All asters are edible, though wild asters are the best to harvest, as the cultivated flowers often seen amid mums (which are incidentally also a member of the Asteraceae family) at pumpkin patches and in ornamental arrangements will typically be sprayed with pesticides and other chemicals. The name *aster*, which is derived from the Ancient Greek for "star," refers to the flower's shape (although it could just as easily hint at the large number of aster species, which seem as numerous as the stars). According to Greek mythology, the flowers grew from the tears of the goddess Astraea, who was heart-broken by the sight of a starless sky.

Asters can be found around the globe, and are especially ubiquitous across the temperate climes. The aster became the symbol of a revolutionary movement in Hungary at the end of World War I when demobilized soldiers in Budapest placed purple asters in their hats to signal their support for the Hungarian National Council.

Musa spp.

Banana Flower

Origin Southern Asia
Type Flowering tree
Blooms Summer

The banana flower hangs like a heart-shaped pendulum from below the last bunch of bananas on the tree.

Banana Flower Thoran
Sri Venudas as told to
Clarisse Demory

The banana flower comes from plantain banana trees. It is said to cleanse the intestines when eaten. It is cooked in Tamil Nadu and Kerala, the two most southerly regions of India. Sri Venudas is from Kerala.

1 cup fresh coconut, grated
6–10 small Indian onions or shallots,
    diced, with 2 sliced into thin rings
1 green chili, chopped, with a third
    sliced into thin rings
1 banana flower
1 tbsp coconut oil
1–2 tsp black mustard seeds
about 15 curry leaves, cleaned and dried
1 tsp turmeric
sea salt

Combine the grated coconut, diced onions, and chopped chili in a grinder and set aside. To prepare the banana flower, holding the stem, remove the dark outer petals until you reach the tender, light-colored petals. Rub some coconut oil on your hands and knife to prevent the sap from sticking, then cut off the stem and chop the inner flower. As you chop, the petals will oxidize and blacken. To prevent blackening, place the chopped petals in water with lemon juice.

Heat the coconut oil in a pan until very hot. Carefully add the mustard seeds to the oil and cook until they pop, taking care not to let them burn. (I suggest covering the pan with a lid. The seeds are naughty and will try to escape!) As soon as the seeds have popped, add the onion and chili rings, the curry leaves, and the chopped banana flower. Combine well, reduce the heat, and cook for about 5 minutes. Add the coconut mixture, turmeric, and salt to taste. Let cook, covered, for 10–15 minutes, adding a little water and stirring as necessary.

Edible Flowers

Ocimum basilicum

Basil

Origin Asia
Type Forb
Blooms Summer

There is a point in late summer when the whole world seems redolent of basil. The plant's oval-shaped leaves remain modest in size year-round as a pot herb until this brief moment when the stalk can grow upwards of two feet tall and tiny white and purple flowers shoot up on long green or purple stems. Markets and gardens become crowded with the leafy herb. This moment can mark the turning of the season and incite a frenzy of pesto-making, a common use for an excess of basil. Caprese salad, another familiar basil preparation, combines the leaf with mozzarella and another late summer delicacy, the tomato.

Basil has inspired poetry and art as much as it has cooking. "She wrapp'd it up, and for its tomb did choose / A garden-pot, wherein she laid it by, / And cover'd it with mould, and o'er it set / Sweet Basil, which her tears kept ever wet," wrote the English poet John Keats in his poem "Isabella, or the Pot of Basil," which in turn inspired two Pre-Raphaelite paintings. Basil's specific epithet, the Latin *basilicum*, comes from the Greek word for "king" or "emperor." In ancient Egypt the herb was used to embalm the holy. By contrast, the Romans believed that the more the plant was abused, the more it would flourish; to encourage an abundant crop, they walked on the plant and, deploying reverse psychology, prayed that it would not vegetate.

Basil is one of the most popular culinary herbs worldwide. It has a warm minty and peppery flavor that allows it to easily accompany cheese and fruit, and both sweet and savory dishes. Its flowers, when consumed, add the same—albeit slightly subtler—herbal spice and are best eaten raw. Like most flowering herbs, the blooms should be harvested prior to seed set to preserve the quality of the coveted leaves.

Image – p. 48

Monarda didyma

Bee Balm

Origin North America
Type Forb
Blooms Summer

Bee balm, also called wild bergamot, is considered a honey plant, a plant that pollinators are deeply attracted to, a quality that has lent it to rewilding efforts in city parks across the United States. Brooklyn Bridge Park, for example, is teeming with the Muppet-like wildflower in late summer. Native to North America and a member of the mint family, Lamiaceae, the bee balm flower stands with a wiry abandon on a tall stalk, its tousled bloom like a feathered headdress.

The name of the flower's genus, *Monarda*, is derived from the Spanish physician and botanist Nicolás Monardes, who catalogued the bee balm in his 1574 survey of plants of the so-called New World. Because it shares the common name bergamot, *Monarda didyma* is often confused with *Citrus bergamia*, a European sour orange that flavors Earl Grey tea. Though the fragrances of their flowers are similar—the reason for the bee balm's other common name—the plants are unrelated. Bee balm was used by Native Americans for medicinal purposes, but was also rubbed on wild game. Its fresh flavor is reminiscent of oregano, and it can be finely chopped and combined with citrus and parsley to make a salsa to accompany fish.

Images – pp. 38, 39

Begonia spp.

Begonia

Origin South America
Type Forb
Blooms Summer

Native to tropical and subtropical climates, the flowers of the genus *Begonia* are globally popular shade plants. Many species and cultivars of begonia are edible, including the wax begonia (*Begonia* × *semperflorens*) and the tuberous begonia (*Begonia* × *tuberhybrida*). Wax begonia flowers, which are commonly pink or orange, grow on short red stems that emerge from waxy, deep green leaves. The flower of the tuberous begonia is more densely petaled and almost resembles a rose. The petals of flowers from both species, though, are characteristically hardy, similar almost to a succulent. The genus name, *Begonia*, is after an intendant of San Domingo (now Hispaniola), Michel Bégon. Begonia flowers are generally eaten fresh to relish their slight lemony zest and satisfying cucumber-like crunch. They pair nicely with fish.

Image – p. 41

Campanula spp.

Bellflower

Origin Europe
Type Forb
Blooms Late spring, summer

The blooms of the bellflower hang in clusters from tall stems, looking like small bluish-purple trumpets. Native to Europe, the plant, whose specific epithets include *rapunculoides* and *rapunculus*, is thought to have inspired the name of the heroine in the folktale "Rapunzel." Its bell-shaped flowers have a storybook quality; one could imagine them being worn as a dress by a fairy. Today the bellflower is considered invasive, as it spreads quickly and can be aggressive when planted in gardens. The entire plant is edible, and its young leaves and flowers have appeared in the cuisines of Nordic and Mediterranean countries. The leaves and flowers have a mild flavor, and can add color to salads, confits, and jellies.

Edible Flowers

Blue butterfly pea flowers grown by Romano
Japitana in his garden in Antipolo, Philippines.

Clitoria ternatea

Blue Butterfly Pea

Origin Africa, Southeast Asia
Type Forb
Blooms Summer

It cannot be confirmed whether Georgia O'Keeffe knew of the blue butterfly pea flower, but in its overt femininity it seems like a bloom she would have been interested to show the world.

    Clitoria ternatea is native to Southeast Asia and Africa, and its appearance is implied by its Latin name, which refers to female genitalia. The blue butterfly pea flower is an electric blue and is sensitive to pH values. When steeped in water, the liquid appears true to the color of the petals. With a bit of lemon juice added, the mixture becomes bright purple. The flower has been employed as a food dye for centuries and is still used widely today as a natural coloring. While the vibrant azure hue is extracted from the flower, it is also edible in full-flower form.

    The blue butterfly pea flower, also known as Asian pigeonwings, is used in traditional Chinese and Ayurvedic medicine to enhance memory and brain function, to relieve stress, and as a calmative agent. In traditional Thai cooking, the flower is used to color sweet and savory foods; it gives *chor muang*, bloom-shaped dumplings, their distinctive violet hue, and it is steeped in water with honey and lemon or lime to make *nam dok anchan*, a butterfly pea flower tea. In Malaysian dishes such as *nasi kerabu*, rice is made sky-blue by adding a few flowers to the pot while cooking.

Image – p. 34

Borage

Seeming to have been plucked directly from a Renaissance painting or a millefleur tapestry, borage has a quality that feels both familiar and foreign, like centuries-old literature brought through the ages. It's easy to imagine these blue flowers floating in a silver goblet of wine in a toast for courage—which is what consuming borage flowers was believed to instill.

The English herbalist John Gerard, in his *The Herbal or General History of Plants* of 1597, wrote, "I, borage, always bring courage," and, indeed, its botanical name, *Borago officinalis*, combines *cor*—"heart"—and *ago*—"I bring." Borage has a long history of imparting bravery, encouraging chivalry, and even bringing happiness. Celtic warriors are said to have indulged in borage wine before going into battle, crusaders drank a tonic of borage flowers, and women secretly added it to the beverages of male suitors to inspire them to propose. It was thought by some to be the source of the drug nepenthe, which was given to Helen to alleviate her sorrow in Homer's *Odyssey*.

Originating in Syria and northern Africa, the plant is now also cultivated throughout the Mediterranean, Asia, Europe, and South America. Appearing at the end of a furry grey stem, its deep blue, star-shaped blossom is pierced through the center with what looks like a tiny pyramidal stake. Though some may find its bristly hairs unpleasant to touch, the flower of the borage is tender, and its clustered petals have a watery, cucumber-like taste. Frozen into ice cubes, the whole flower can be added to lemonade, white wine sangria, and spritzers. It also integrates naturally into salads and cold soups, can be stuffed along with ricotta into pastas such as pansotti, ravioli, or agnolotti, and can even be added to brine when making pickles.

Images – pp. 37, 40, 57

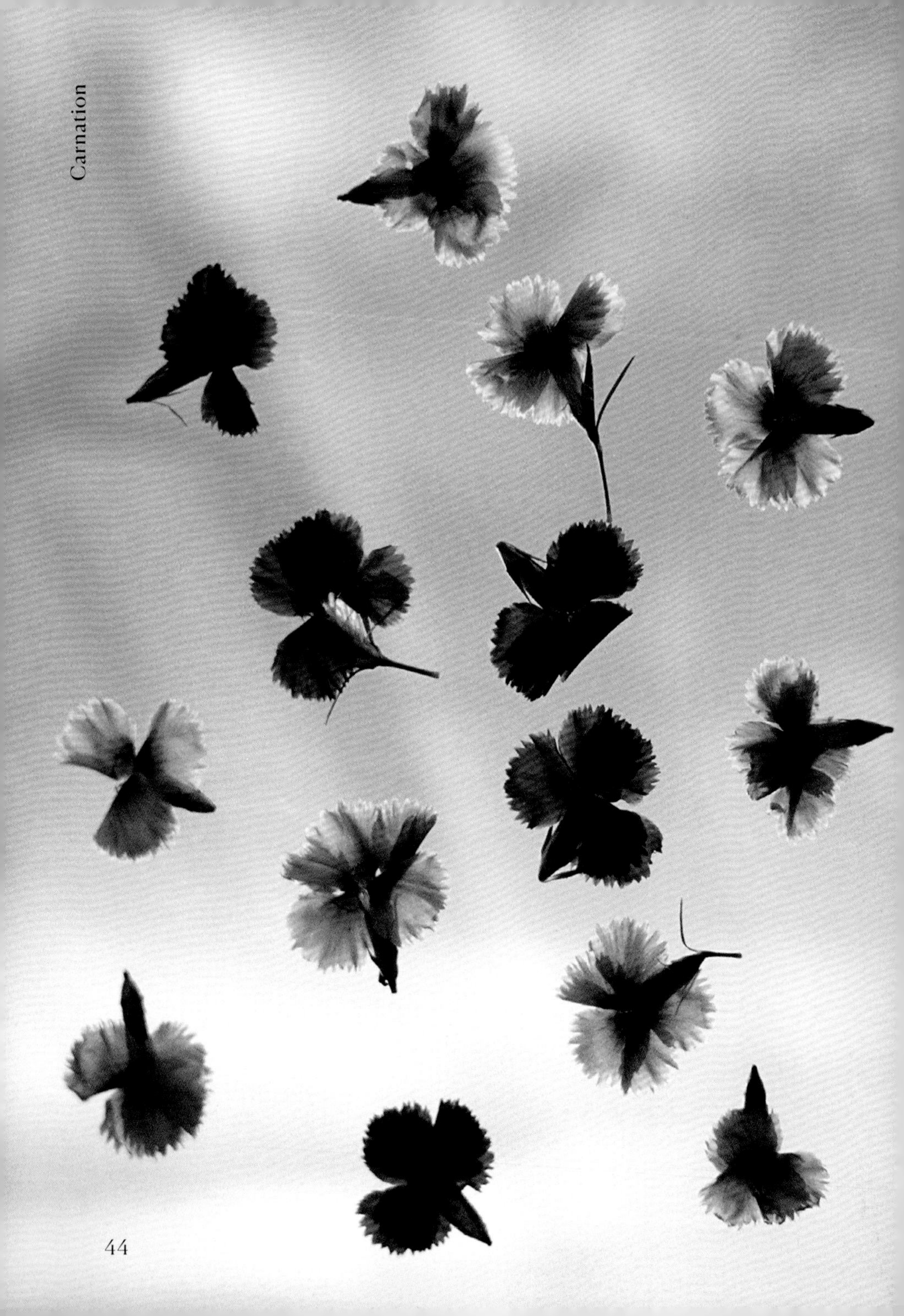

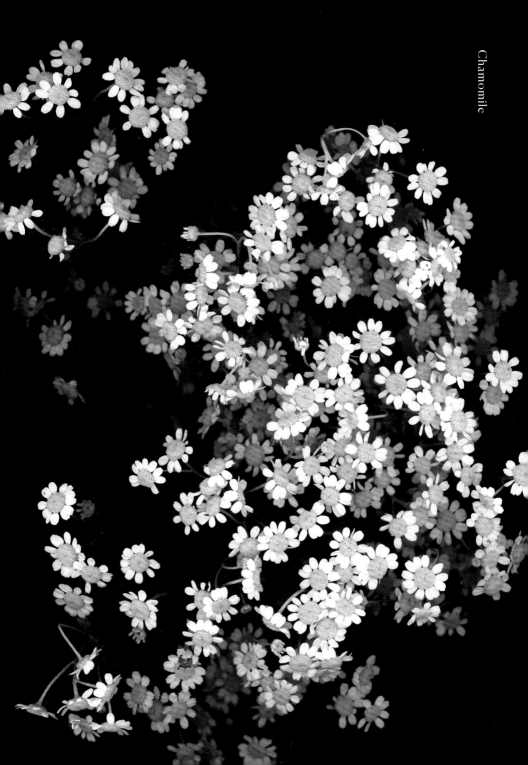

Chamomile

47

Bougainvillea

Origin South America
Type Flowering vine
Blooms Year-round

Pronouncing bougainvillea is always a fun game. Try: *boo-gan-vil-leah!* The bougainvillea's thick vines and vivid pink flowers cascade from trellises and blanket sun-baked stone walls in hot climates. It is the plant's large papery bracts—modified leaves—not its flowers' petals, that are bright magenta. On closer inspection you'll see the bracts protecting one to three small tubular flowers.

It is said that Jeanne Baret, the eighteenth-century French botanist who disguised herself as a man—Jean Baret—in order to join Louis-Antoine de Bougainville's expedition in the 1760s, was in fact the first European to spot and formally document the flower that would become known as bougainvillea, in addition to being the first woman to complete a circumnavigation of the globe in the name of botany.

The flower bracts of the bougainvillea are edible and can be eaten fresh or steeped in tea, or even made into an *agua fresca*, as Aurora Robles describes on page 50.

Image – p. 50

Bougainvillea Agua Fresca
(*Agua fresca de bugambilia*)
Aurora Robles

For many Mexicans, there is nothing more redolent of the country than an *agua fresca*. Translated literally it means "fresh water," but its colloquial meaning is any kind of fruit, flower, or seed, steeped or blended with plenty of water, then strained and sweetened to produce an infinity of flavors that vary based on the seasonality of the fruit or flower, or the region in Mexico in which the drink is consumed. The most widely known *agua fresca* of the floral variety is *agua de Jamaica*, which can easily be found in traditional Mexican restaurants or food trucks in the United States these days. A more rarely seen *agua fresca* is made of bougainvillea, boiled or steeped, sometimes using both fresh and dried flowers (the piercing purple variety is said to produce the most intense color).

Most recipes for bougainvillea tea note its health benefits, from reducing fever to treating a dry cough. It is often mixed with lime juice, and to be honest, the lime flavor does prevail, and one is left wondering if the healing lies in the innate pleasure of drinking that inimitable hue, so evocative of summers under the hot sun in Mexico and California.

After collecting a few branches of bougainvillea (aim for anywhere from 20–30 flowers), snip the flowers off the branch and remove the calyx. (It is sometimes white and looks like another smaller flower sitting inside the pink, papery petals holding the stamen and pistils. It can impart bitterness, so it is best removed.) Rinse the flowers and set them aside to dry. Depending on the heat and humidity, this can take between one and four days. The dried flowers are said to intensify the hue of the drink.

Bring 5 cups of water to boil, and add the dried flowers. Lower the heat and let the flowers steep for about 15 minutes. If you are curious to try the brew at this point, it has a very lightly herbal flavor.

Add a sweetener of your choice to taste (if using cane sugar or honey, add while the liquid is still warm to dissolve the sweetener thoroughly). Let cool. Add the juice of 4 to 6 limes (about 1/2 cup) to the cooled and sweetened "tea."

Serve the *agua fresca* chilled or over ice and garnish with dried bougainvillea or a slice of lime.

Edible Flowers

Eriogonum fasciculatum

Buckwheat

Origin Americas
Type Flowering shrub
Blooms Summer

From each slim stem of California buckwheat pops a globe of tiny pink-and-white blossoms that mature into a deep red when ready for harvest. Native to the American Southwest and to northwestern Mexico, California buckwheat, a species of wild buckwheat, is most commonly seen today blooming in Coastal California. Though it is a different species from *Fagopyrum esculentum*, the pseudocereal used to make porridge or soba noodles, California buckwheat is edible. It is a common food crop in Native American cooking, used to make tea and, with the seeds extracted from the dried flowers and ground into a flour, to bake bread. California buckwheat is also very attractive to pollinators and an important source of honey.

Acmella oleracea

Buzz Button

Origin South America
Type Forb
Blooms Year-round

Eating a buzz button feels like soda on your tongue, or like Pop Rocks. A sensation that is generally associated with the unnatural or manufactured is all the more surprising from an ancient flower. Believed to be native to Peru and Brazil, the oval-shaped yellow blossom is dense and tough to chew at first, but alchemizes with saliva as its breaks down, producing a frothy, electrifying, buzzing sensation. As it sits on the tongue, it slowly softens and becomes digestible. Also known as Szechuan button and electric button, the buzz button has been widely used for its analgesic properties and its innate numbing quality; it has been a treatment for toothaches for centuries. Buzz button's delicately citrusy, grassy flavor balances out with a cooling finish—like toothpaste. The flower is a lively addition to cocktails with cucumber, lemon verbena, or elderflower.

Image – p. 42

Calendula officinalis

Calendula

Origin Europe
Type Forb
Blooms Summer

Calendula has become a faddish ingredient in healing salves and lotions, but its roots are ancient. Early Christians called this flower Mary's gold (it is still commonly confused with the marigold, p. 144) and placed it by statues of the Virgin Mary. Calendula is also considered the most sacred flower of ancient India, its blooms adorning holy statues and altars in wreaths and garlands. Perhaps this is because calendula's rayed flowers are heliotropic—looking always to the sun.

Native to Europe and perhaps parts of the Middle East, today calendula is cultivated worldwide. As its genus name, *Calendula* from *wor calendae*, meaning "throughout the months," implies, it is a hardy flower. A member of the Aster family, calendula is sometimes called pot marigold due to the similarity of its appearance with the marigold, but it is an entirely different plant. Its bright yellow petals, sought after for both pigment and flavor, have been used culinarily for centuries. In ancient Egypt it was considered the "poor man's saffron," and would be employed to color foods for a fraction of the price. The Romans mixed calendula with vinegar to season their meat dishes and vegetables. The slight bitterness of the blossoms goes well with sweet desserts featuring honey, or including coconut or other tropical fruits. Calendula can be an economical substitute for saffron (p. 198) in paella.

Images – pp. 46, 53

Calendula

Edible Flowers

Camellia

Edible Flowers

Camellia

Origin Asia
Type Flowering shrub
Blooms Early spring

Thousands of years ago, in ancient China (as the story goes), a weary monk put a pot of water on to boil for soup. Leaves of a flowering plant fell into the pot, the monk drank the water and felt invigorated, thus inventing tea; the species, *Camellia sinensis*, tea plant, contains a small amount of caffeine and is still used to make most teas, from black tea to green tea to oolong.

Another species of the genus *Camellia*, *Camellia japonica*, which has the common name camellia, has also inspired creative invention. French author and playwright Alexandre Dumas's 1848 novel *La Dame aux Camélias*, which was later adapted for the theater, tells the story of a courtesan who wore a white camellia when she was available to her lovers and a red camellia when she was menstruating. Coco Chanel, who as a girl attended a performance of the play starring actress Sarah Bernhardt, would wear a white camellia herself and later emblazon the flower on her couture designs. The white camellia was also adopted by the women's suffrage movement in New Zealand, and appears on its ten-dollar note.

Native to Southeast Asia, plants of the genus *Camellia* have found their way to most parts of the world, even flowering year-round in mild winter climates. In North America, *Camellia japonica* is most common in the southern United States. First arriving in the colonies from Portugal and France, the flowers are still prominent in cities such as Savannah, where their large blooms drip from dark green bushes—as if the weight of their languid beauty draws them to the ground. The American South has also used the camellia to recast its own troubled history. Magnolia Plantation, in Charleston, opened its garden to the public during Reconstruction. Today, the plantation's garden is home to the oldest and largest collection of camellias in the United States.

The elegant camellia flower is often seen as a garnish on wedding cakes. The petals can also be candied or tossed in a fruit salad, adding a pop of color and sweetness.

Images – pp. 45, 54

Capparis spinose

Caper

Origin Australia, southern Eurasia
Type Flowering shrub
Blooms Summer

The caper is perhaps most familiar for its bud: in several Mediterra-nean cuisines, particularly Italian, these tiny, dark green, tightly closed immature flowers are salted or pickled and add a bright note to meat dishes, salads, and pasta sauces; capers are an essential ingredient in *spaghetti alla puttanesca*, for example. But, if allowed to bloom, the caper flower lives an entirely different life: often found growing wild from sun-warmed stone walls, the caper bush flower's crepe-like white petals open to reveal a delightful spray of purple stamens. The blossoms are delicate and fragrant white flowers, but, as with the arti-choke, their appearance signals the overripening of the most edible part of the plant.

Carum carvi

Caraway

Origin Eurasia, northern Africa
Type Forb
Blooms Summer

The seeds of the caraway might be the most familiar part of the plant, but its flowers are also edible. The caraway bears tiny, white, daisylike blossoms that grow in umbels—umbrella-like constellations of flowers at the ends of stalks growing from a single point—like flowers of the carrot plant (another member of the Apiaceae family). The flowers can be used in ways similar to the seeds—that is, baked into bread, pickled with cabbage and cucumbers, or sprinkled as an accompaniment on cured or cooked fish—but in contrast to the sharp, nutty, licorice taste of its seeds, the flowers will impart a much milder flavor.

Borage and chamomile found in Longwood
Gardens in Pennsylvania.

Elettaria cardamomum

Cardamom

Origin India
Type Forb
Blooms Spring

Consuming cardamom provides a synesthetic experience: it tastes like the color dusty rose, and smells brighter and peppery, as if a reddish-yellow is also emerging. In a way, cardamom is a tiny sunrise of a spice. It has the unique ability to be both cooling and warming. When added to coffee and savory and sweet dishes, it manages to both complement and rise above. Its flavor is powerful and only a tiny amount is needed when cooking or baking. The cardamom seeds grow in small green pods. Crack one open and ground the dried seed to extract the most flavor. The whole, closed pod can also be steeped and mixed with aromatic herbs and flowers to make chai or other teas.

The cardamom plant is native to India and has been extensively recorded in Ayurvedic literature. It remains an integral ingredient in Indian cooking. Cardamom is often paired with pistachio and rose (p. 193), but can be added to poultry dishes and to curries. Cardamom is also prominent in Scandinavian baking. The cardamom plant produces a white flower with fine fuchsia veins that radiate from its center. The flowers blossom in spring before the seed is fully formed in the fall. The blossoms are edible and can be harvested and eaten separately or added as pretty decorative elements to cardamom-scented dishes.

Dianthus caryophyllus

Carnation

Origin Mediterranean
Type Forb
Blooms Late spring

When Vita Sackville-West, English writer, garden designer, and lover of Virginia Woolf, wrote of flowers—which she did often—she always had kind words for the carnation. Today, in its ubiquity in supermarket bouquets, the ruffled flower can be unassuming, as unremarkable as the greenery used for filler. However, the carnation has a long and dynamic history. According to Christian symbolism, the flower first sprang from the tears of the Virgin Mary as she witnessed the plight of Jesus; etymologically speaking, carnation is closely related to "Incarnation," the union of the human and the divine in the form of her son. In Leonardo da Vinci's painting *The Madonna of the Carnation*, Mary offers a blood-red carnation to the holy baby. The flower's name also could refer to "coronation," from the Latin *coronare*, alluding to flower garlands such as those worn in ancient Greek ceremonies.

Over the centuries, the flower has taken on other meanings. Oscar Wilde endorsed green carnations as a symbol of homosexuality in 1892 when he and friends began to wear the flower in their lapels. This was immortalized in the novel *The Green Carnation* by writer and satirist Robert Hichens and later in the song "We All Wear Green Carnations," written by Noel Coward for his operetta *Bitter Sweet*. The red carnation has represented various labor movements and was the emblem of the 1974 Carnation Revolution in Lisbon, so called as pacifist activist Celeste Caeiro, a restaurant worker, gave carnations to soldiers engaged in a coup, who put the flowers in the muzzles of their guns.

The petals of the carnation, which grow in fragrant, loose tufts, have a slightly spicy, clove-like flavor (another of its common names is clove pink). The flower is thought to be among the over one hundred plants used to make Chartreuse, the acid-green French liqueur. Add chopped carnation flowers to rice dishes or salads. Whole blooms may be simmered with sugar and water to make a pink carnation syrup.

Image – p. 44

Matricaria chamomilla

Chamomile

Origin Europe
Type Forb
Blooms Summer

The flower of the chamomile, daisylike with its rays of white petals surrounding a sunny yellow button center, is today most commonly consumed in tea. The small flower seems delicate and dainty, but is quite hardy and has a powerful herbal presence when eaten fresh or dried. The wildflower, native to Southern and Eastern Europe, has been harvested for centuries as a medicinal herb. The flower's common name comes from the Ancient Greek for "ground apple" because of its strong fruity fragrance—an aroma evoking the scent of fermented apple. This quality links it to hops, the fruit of the hop plant (p. 127) *Humulus lupulus*, as chamomile it thought to have been among the herbs and spices often combined into gruit, a mixture used to flavor beer before hops. The small blooms maintain their flavor when incorporated into cooking. Chamomile, both fresh and dried, can be infused into sugary creams, baked into cakes, or added to homemade granola.

Images — pp. 47, 57, 61, 215

Miso Soup with Chamomile
Heidi Swanson

I love chamomile and have been harvesting a lot of the flowers from my garden and making a simple but strong, extra-hot tea with it. There are many things you can use the chamomile tea for other than simply drinking it. I've been adding it to soups. After I strain the chamomile flowers, I add the hot tea to a miso base, which mixes nicely. The sweetness of the flower counters the saltiness of the miso.

It is a very simple soup that can be enjoyed on its own, or you can add vegetables or tofu to make it a bit heartier. Orange and lemon zest can also be added to the hot broth for a little more complexity of flavor. And a few flowers, dried or fresh, make a nice embellishment.

Oh! And don't forget to add a big shower of chives to the soup.

Dried chamomile

Edible Flowers

Cherry blossom

Prunus spp.

Cherry Blossom

Origin Eurasia
Type Flowering tree
Blooms Spring

For about a month in early spring, the world erupts into small pink blossoms. The blooming of cherry trees, in gardens and lining thoroughfares, signals the end of winter. The flowering trees are especially important in Japan, where they are known as *sakura*. The custom of *hanami*—"flower viewing"—for which people flock to see the flowers, picnic, and drink sake beneath the trees, is one of the most cherished traditions of Japanese culture. The stunning display is short-lived: each tree only blooms for up to two weeks, during which the petals carpet the ground beneath it in a pale pink snow. The ephemeral nature of the flower is integral to its symbolism and was best articulated by Motoori Norinaga, an eighteenth-century Japanese scholar who associated the Shinto concept of *mono no aware*, or the "pathos of things," with the flower. Of the flowers he wrote, "If I were asked to explain the Japanese spirit, I would say it is wild cherry blossoms glowing in the morning sun." The cherry blossom represents the impermanence of being and the grace of accepting mortality, an idea that has filtered through all channels of popular culture in Japan, from literature and film to pop music. *Sakura* gardens may be found in almost every major city in the world; in 1912, Tokyo mayor Yukio Ozaki gave more than three thousand cherry trees to Washington, DC. Now celebrated worldwide, cherry blossom festivals draw on the brevity and captivating quality of the coordinated bloom.

When eaten, the flowers are inevitably floral and slightly sweet, with a tang. In Japan, the blossoms and leaves are often pickled in ume vinegar and added to sweets such as *hanami dango*, dumplings made for *hanami*. The blossoms can be steeped in wine or drunk as a tea. They are also beautiful suspended in pink jelly atop *panna cotta*.

Images – pp. 62, 75

Cichorium intybus

Chicory

Origin Europe
Type Forb
Blooms Late summer

Long before the craft-roasted brews of today, chicory brought its
woody richness to coffee cups the world over. Chicory's origins as a
comestible date back to the ancient world. It was consumed in Egypt
and was mentioned by the Roman poet Horace as a staple in his simple
diet. It was first recorded in the seventeenth century as a cultivated
plant, and later the roots of the chicory were used as an additive or
substitute for coffee, especially when coffee beans were prohibitively
expensive or scarce—as in Napoleonic France during the Continental
System blockade. But should you think chicory's nutty flavor is only
something to be tolerated, know that it is relished. Coffee with chicory
is widely drunk in India, France, Turkey, Lebanon, and Greece, among
many other places. Though chicory was first added to coffee in New
Orleans because of shortages during the Civil War, chicory coffee—
traditionally drunk as café au lait—has since become an iconic beverage
synonymous with the city.

 Throughout late summer and into early fall, chicory can be seen
growing wild across Europe and the United States—even as a roadside
weed in New York City. A member of the Asteraceae family—which
makes it a cousin to the sunflower (p. 207), the aster (p. 29), the dandelion (p. 93), the dahlia (p. 89), and many, many other flowering plants—its
periwinkle-blue blooms have rays of petals edged in a zigzag pattern, as
if trimmed by pinking shears. The flower's life is brief, lasting only one
day, so pick them while you can and add them to cultured butter or toss
the petals in a salad.

Image — p. 76

A Cake of Flowers

My daughter Red's first birthday was April 18, 2020. We had been living through the pandemic for over a month, but we were still grasping onto the illusion that this would be a brief pause, a time-out more than a new reality. It took a family milestone for the gravity of the situation to set in.

We had moved to Los Angeles a few months prior, and our world was upside down, even before the global shit hit the fan. I ached for the life I had left in New York, but I found solace in long walks, lonely as they were, around my neighborhood of Montecito Heights. Following the desolate, dried-up concrete ditch we call the LA "river," I found secret urban staircases and moments of quiet nature in the middle of the city. I made loops with the stroller, filling the undercarriage with pilfered treasures, drawing a map in my mind of which homes had fruit trees with branches that extended over property lines. I was comforted by the silly idea that in the apocalypse, my family might be saved by a forager's access to the most delicious avocados, guavas, Oro Blanco grapefruits, and miner's lettuce that money could buy. And while we anticipated the end of days, I could comfortably skip a trip to the grocery store because the stinging nettles had just popped up and we would now be having homemade forest-green ravioli for dinner, even if we were rationing flour.

In an effort to make the most of Red's birthday, my husband leaned into the production of a Zoom party. He choreographed the whole thing, setting up multiple cameras and sets for the party to travel through. It would commence with a jam session in the living room, musical instruments on a sheepskin rug, in a field of tropical foliage and bird of paradise filched from the abandoned lot nearby. The grand finale would take place in a corner of the dining room, the high chair engulfed in a sea of balloons. There, Red would dig into her cake.

Overwhelmed and alienated by the AV logistics, I leaned into the making of a cake. I baked baby-friendly layers made with oat and almond flour, sweetened only with banana. I sandwiched garden strawberries inside and topped it all with fluffy clouds of Greek yogurt coconut frosting. The decoration would be a ridiculous amount of edible flowers, all of them sourced within a three-block radius of our home. Nasturtiums of all colors clung to the cement retaining wall across the street. Calendula grew around the base of the loquat tree on the curb. The community garden planted sweet peas along their border, and I snipped a few (not proud of that, but a desperate mom will go to great lengths for her child). I planted blue-and-white borage in my front yard, and sprinkled the mild blossoms on top. It was stunning.

The Zoom party was a failure. I have never felt so alone in the presence of over a hundred close friends and family. Red was unable to focus on her instruments and just pawed desperately at the screen, trying to connect with the two-dimensional people who mimed and gesticulated on mute. When it came to the cake, she regained her focus, digging her hands into my masterpiece, gleefully smearing it all over her face. My husband and I cried once the Zoom gathering was over, really feeling the isolation and the immense distance between us and the people we love. Looking back now, it was just the beginning of what would prove to be the most challenging time of our lives.

Later that night, I found some solace in the pictures of the cake I had taken on my phone, imagining Red feeling proud of my efforts, the way I still do when I see the four-by-six photos of my first birthday cakes, each of them a masterpiece by Mom.

Chrysanthemum spp.

Chrysanthemum

Origin Asia
Type Forb
Blooms Fall

When hot water is poured over a whole dried chrysanthemum, it blossoms again as a tea. Submerged, the petals expand and appear magnified, like a small sun glowing gold. Indeed, chrysanthemum's name is derived from the Greek for "gold"—*chrysos*—and "flower"—*anthemon* (though chrysanthemums can be found in a range of colors, from yellow and orange to red and deep purple). In Japan, the golden flower, known as *kiku*, stands as the imperial seal. It also marks the changing of seasons as the bright light of summer mellows and deepens with the approach of autumn, inspiring festivals and ornate sculptural arrangements that emulate the sun. In South Korea, rice wine made with chrysanthemum, called *gukhwaju*, is typically drunk on the celebration that marks the Double Ninth Festival, the ninth day of the ninth month.

Like the daylily (p. 94), the chrysanthemum has been consumed in China for centuries. It was initially cultivated as a culinary herb, and all varieties are still edible. The petals are tangy and slightly bitter, but range in taste from faintly peppery to a mildly vegetal flavor that some liken to cauliflower. Prior to cooking, remove the petals from the base of the flower. The leaves are most flavorful and can be used to enliven vinegars or blanched to prepare *goma-ae*, a Japanese dish with greens in a sweet soy and mirin dressing sprinkled with sesame seeds. The flower and its leaves can also be cooked into hot pot.

Images — pp. 43, 83

Coriandrum sativum

Cilantro

Origin Eurasia, North Africa
Type Forb
Blooms Summer

Cilantro is older than recorded time. To our knowledge, it has been cultivated for over eight thousand years. Dried pieces of the plant found in the Nahal Hemar Cave in Israel, which dates to the early Neolithic, are considered the oldest archaeological discovery of the species. *Coriandrum sativum* is native to southwest Asia and North Africa and today is an herb that is found across the globe. Its other common names include coriander (which in North America refers specifically to the plant's seeds) and Chinese parsley. Despite its presence in international cuisines, cilantro has a reputation as a divisive herb. To many, it tastes delicate, herbal, floral, and bright; to others it is bitter and soapy. Both are true assessments, as chemists have found specific compounds present in the plant that are similar to those in lotions and soaps. A genetic disposition leads some to detect these compounds more strongly than others.

All of the soft leafy parts of the herb are edible, including the petite, lacy white flowers that blossom in clusters. Cilantro flowers taste like a milder version of their leaves, but impart a lemony note. The blossoms may be added to any recipe that calls for the leaves or, for a milder flavor, as a substitute. Cilantro has a cooling effect in spicy dishes and lifts rich, savory foods with its brightness. The leaves and flowers suit fish, chicken, salad, pasta, and broths, and pair well with ingredients such as avocado, carrots, zucchini, tomato, coconut milk, citrus, ginger, mint, lemongrass, chili peppers, and yogurt. Both blossoms and leaves are best added at the very end, and always fresh as they lose flavor with exposure to heat.

Images – pp. 69, 80

Cilantro and gem marigold

Edible Flowers

Citrus blossom

Edible Flowers

Citrus spp.

Citrus Blossom

Origin Asia
Type Flowering tree
Blooms Late winter, early spring

All citrus trees produce similar flowers that appear in clusters alongside the fruit: each waxy white blossom bears five petals and a cylindrical, crown-like center that seems to have gilded edges. From the dense flowers wafts a strong, concentrated, and intoxicating fragrance.

The citrus blossom with the most significance both culinarily and symbolically is the orange blossom. Associated with purity, chastity, and fertility, orange blossoms were part of wedding rituals in China. In 1840, in England, Queen Victoria would wed Prince Albert wearing a wreath of orange blossoms, setting a trend among Victorian brides for jewelry in the shape of the flower. According to fashion historian Cornelia Powell, the queen's floral adornment made such an impact that "to gather orange blossoms" came to mean "to seek a wife."

In the Mediterranean region, the blossoms of the bitter orange, *Citrus aurantium,* have since at least the eight century been pressed to produce neroli oil, an essential oil still widely used as a component in many perfumes. Orange blossom water, made by distilling the flowers, is essential to Middle Eastern cuisine and can be used in baking and cooking in ways similar to rose water. Incorporated into desserts, the essence adds a sweet, tangy, floral flavor. Orange blossom water is commonly called for in Moroccan recipes; it is combined with almond paste in cookies and is an indispensable ingredient in *bastilla,* the sweet and savory chicken pie.

"Citrus trees are evergreen, and in the ancient world they were coveted for their beauty long before anyone ever thought to eat their fruit," writes John McPhee in his book *Oranges.* In the orange groves of Florida, at times the air is perfumed by millions of the blossoms. McPhee remarks on the beauty of the groves through the words of an eighth-century Chinese poet:

> In the full of spring on the banks of a river—
> Two big gardens planted with thousands of orange trees.
> Their thick leaves are putting the clouds to shame.

Images – pp. 70, 78, 79

Trifolium spp.

Clover

Origin Eurasia
Type Forb
Blooms Summer

To be "in clover" is to be carefree and comfortable, like a cow in a clover field. The clover's stem creeps along the ground and can grow to a foot or more, producing a mass of three-part (or if you're lucky, four-part) leaves and small spherical flowers. The flowers of the white clover, *Trifolium repens,* are colored in ombré progressions of white to pink or purple; the red clover, *Trifolium pratense,* from pale pink near the center to a deep fuchsia. The flowers are short-lived and have a sweet, anise-like, vaguely vanilla flavor. They can be brewed for tea, churned into ice cream, or dried and mixed into cookies. Once the flowers begin to turn brown, they are inedible.

Image – p. 77

Celosia spp.

Cockscomb

Origin Africa
Type Forb
Blooms Late summer

The appearance of cockscomb, flowers of the genus *Celosia,* can be confounding, as if they belong undersea, not on land. Celosia plants bear three forms of flowers: one is small and flame-like, another is woollier and recalls a campfire, and the third is velvety and resembles a brain. The most commonly eaten is cockscomb, a bloom native to Africa and an ingredient found in cuisines throughout that continent and in Asia. When young and tender, the entire plant, including its flowers, can be added to soups or stews or simply sautéed with salt and pepper and served on its own as a side dish. Celosia flowers may also be steeped in hot water to create a bright pink tea.

Image – p. 73

Dwarf Mallow

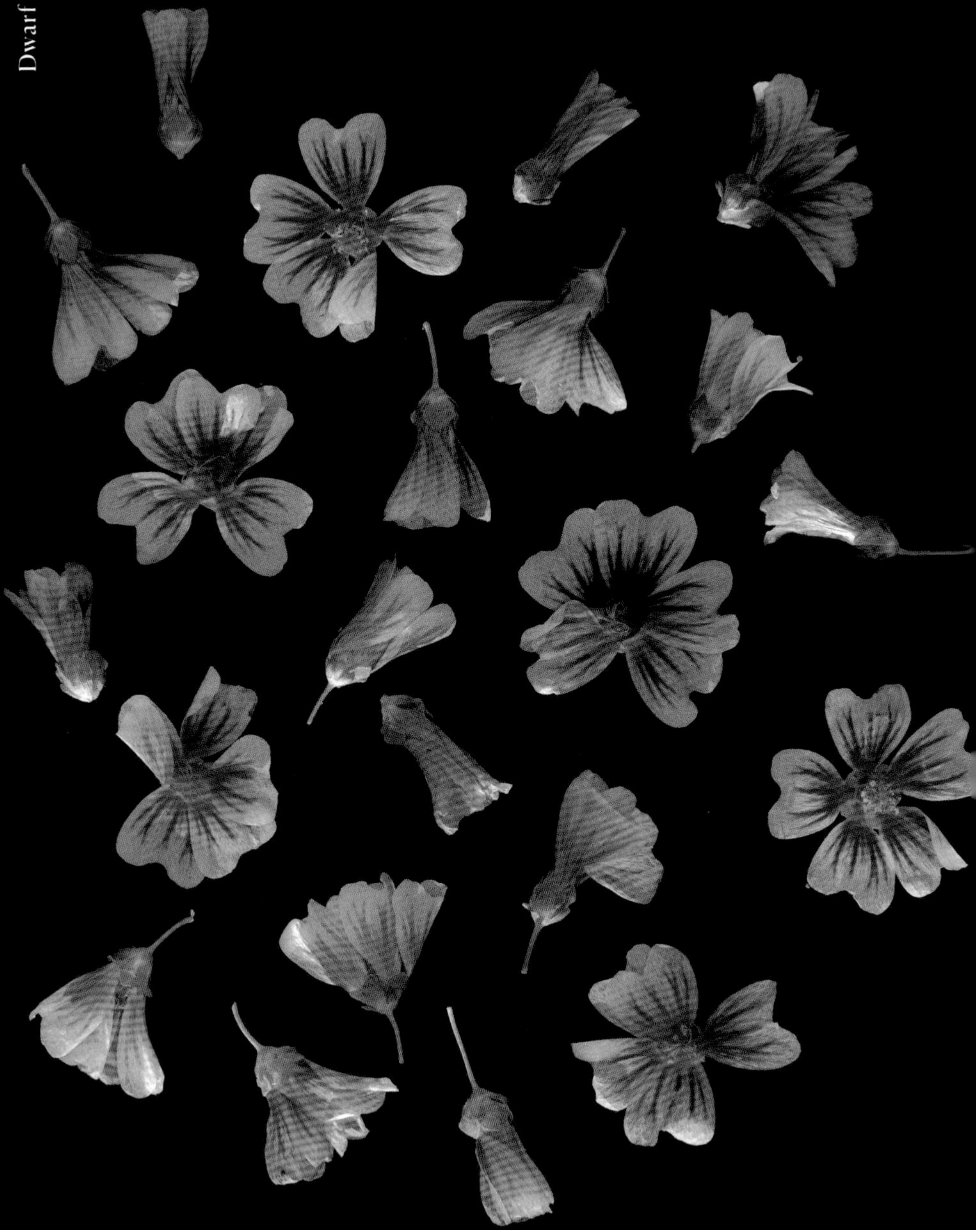

Citrus Blossom

Centaurea cyanus

Cornflower

Origin Europe
Type Forb
Blooms Summer

The blue of the cornflower persists. Even when left in direct sunlight for months, its stem withers to a sepia while its bloom remains vibrant. The flower's most common color is an Yves Klein–blue—matte and potent. As the story goes, archaeologists discovered a wreath of cornflowers beside an alabaster cup in the tomb of Tutankhamen, the Egyptian boy king who died around 1324 BCE. The flowers were still blue.

A cobalt shade is the rarest in nature, but it is said that centuries ago the cornflower was so abundant in Europe that entire meadows were covered with the wildflower. Its perseverance and prominence has given the cornflower many names and a reputation as a symbol of freedom and romance. *Centaurea cyanus* received its genus name from the centaur Chiron, who, according to Greek mythology, imparted knowledge of medicinal herbs to humankind. Its specific epithet, *cyanus*, is after an admirer of Flora, the Roman goddess of spring, who would bring the goddess wreaths of the flower. In Great Britain, the cornflower is sometimes called the bluet, and in France, *bleuet*. The tattered look of the flower's petals is believed to be the reason the plant is sometimes known as ragged sailor or ragged robin. Another common name, bachelor's button, likely originated from a Victorian-era custom of men placing the flower in a buttonhole of their jacket to signal their availability. In twentieth-century America, the cornflower would become associated with the Kennedy family, as it was President John F. Kennedy's favorite flower; cornflowers adorned the wedding party of his daughter Caroline, and later his son John would wear a cornflower boutonniere for his own nuptial ceremony.

The cornflower can grow up to three feet tall, its papery, pointed outer florets blooming in layered rays on thin, resilient stems. It is commonly packaged in commercially available edible flower mixes. The flavor of the cornflower is subtly spiced and sweet. It can be baked into cookies, sprinkled on salads, and pressed into fresh pasta.

Images — pp. 4, 84

Cosmos spp.

Cosmos

Origin The Americas
Type Forb
Blooms Summer

Similar to the super blooms of the California desert or *hanami*—cherry blossom viewing parties—in Japan, in South Korea a change of seasons is marked by the flowering of cosmos. In fall, the enchanting flower bursts from parks and blankets fields. On Hajungdo Island in the city of Daegu, visitors during the first couple weeks of September can view the nearly one thousand square meters of flower fields abounding with cosmos. In Guri, just outside of Seoul, a festival dedicated to the flower is held each fall.

    Cosmos sulphureus, the bright orange and yellow variety, is one of the only edible species of cosmos, and the whole plant many be eaten. Native to the Americas, the plant's flowers can grow up to two inches in diameter, bear two tiers of oval-shaped petals, bloom in wild bunches, and attract butterflies in droves. Another edible species of cosmos, *Cosmos caudatus*, appears in the cuisines of Malaysia—where it is called *ulam raja*, "king's salad"—and Indonesia—where it is known as *kenikir*.

Cucumis sativus

Cucumber

Origin India
Type Flowering vine
Blooms Summer

Before the tendriled, creeping vine of the cucumber plant bears its familiar fruit, it produces bright yellow, five-petaled flowers. The flowers bloom for only one day and fall off as the cucumber fruit grows. Harvest them while you can to add a crisp bite to salads or fish dishes, use them as a refreshing garnish for summer cocktails, or brine them in vinegar, along with the cucumber fruit, to add color to your pickle jar.

Image – p.81

Edible Flowers

Blessings on the
Forest Floor

In Hindu cosmology, in the gardens of paradise belonging to Lord
Indra, the Hindu king of the gods, atop the sacred Mount Meru, and
guarded by celestial beings, grows a tree. Nondescript in appearance,
it is powerful in its significance. Known as the *Kalpavriskha*, Sanskrit
for "tree of life," it is a wish-granting tree. One of the earthly
equivalents of this primordial tree, which selflessly serves the tribals
in the heartlands of India by providing them with food, fuel, and
fodder, is the flowering mahua (*Madhuca longifolia*).

Dotted across the jungles of the central Indian states of Madhya
Pradesh, Odisha, and Chhattisgarh, the mahua blooms in the harshest
of seasons, the Indian summer, when a hot, dry wind called the *loo*
blows across the region, sapping life and moisture from the otherwise
dense, luxuriant vegetation. While green forests turn brown and brittle
overnight and crops begin to fail, the mahua blossoms, and its fleshy,
berry-like yellow flowers fall to the ground every night, waiting to
be collected. Every part of the tree is useful, but none as much as the
flowers, on which humans and animals such as elephants, bears, and
monkeys survive in long months of scarcity.

The mahua tastes of the earthiness of hardship, the sharpness of ingenuity, and the sweetness of a gift from the gods. Its heady, sickly sweet smell hangs in the air throughout the summer. Dried mahua flowers are ground into flour and can be mixed with wheat flour and other grains to make steamed cakes and breads, like the *latta* in Madhya Pradesh, *asur khichdi* in Chhattisgarh, and the *mahua poda pitha* in Odisha. It is deep-fried and made into fritters or eaten raw as a snack. It is made into spicy pickles, syrupy jams, and traditional desserts like *halwa*, *kheer*, and *laddoos*. Mahua raita, a yogurt-based dip, makes a refreshing, sweet-and-salty condiment. The flowers are rich in phosphorus, iron, and calcium and are so sweet that they are sometimes used as a replacement for sugar; the name *mahua* comes from the Sanksrit word *madhu*, meaning "honey."

Despite its culinary versatility, mahua is best known for the potent, fiery liquor brewed from its flowers, the only distilled spirit made from a sweet flower in the world. The Indian sloth bear—immortalized as the bumbling Baloo in Rudyard Kipling's *The Jungle Book*—is a mahua aficionado and can often be found roaming the jungles of Madhya Pradesh, on which Kipling based the landscape of the book, in a state of mild intoxication from eating too many mahua flowers.

But for all its sacred and storied history, the mahua flower is not a delicacy. It is being rapidly replaced by "civilized" foods like rice and wheat, and the generous mahua, food of sustenance, now sometimes leaves an aftertaste of shame even among tribals. But as a *Kalpavriksha*, the mahua blossoms eternally on earth as it does in paradise, waiting patiently to fulfill the wishes of those in need. Humans or animals— they need only ask.

Dahlia pinnata

Dahlia

Origin Mexico, Central America
Type Forb
Blooms Summer, fall

The dahlia is today not well known as an edible flower, though long before it was brought to Holland and developed into many of the ornamental varieties seen today, the dahlia was a food crop native to the Americas. Originally found in the mountain regions of Mexico and Central America, the dahlia is a relative of the tuberous sunflower (aka the sunchoke or Jerusalem artichoke, which is in fact native to North America), and like its cousin, the dahlia produces tubers that resemble small potatoes. In 1570 the dahlia was documented by Spanish conquistadors and specimens of the flower were sent Spain. There the dahlia was given its common name by Antonio José Cavanilles, a botanist and director of the Royal Botanical Garden of Madrid, who christened the flower after the Swedish botanist Anders Dahl.

Dahlia flowers come in white and rich shades of yellow, orange, red, pink, and purple. The petals are crisp, and the flavor of the flower is mild and grassy, likened to water chestnut. The dahlia is often used to decorate cakes and other desserts, but can be served with cheese as an edible garnish. Dahlia petals can also bring some color to grain or green salads or to a salsa for fish.

Daisy

Bellis perennis

Daisy

Origin Europe
Type Forb
Blooms Spring, summer

During the Renaissance, a rise in humanist philosophy positioned food as a pleasure, which was a shift from the medieval associations of food with gluttony and lust. Flowers became accepted into people's everyday diets, and in fifteenth-century England even the poorest of the country were eating salads of daisies, borage (p. 36) , violets (p. 213), and herbs. If any one flower could represent a humanist ideology, the daisy it would be, with its single ray of white petals open to the world. We imagine children plucking daisies to make flower crowns, a gentle reminder of play and discovery. And there is no shortage of daisy as it grows in wild abundance, dusting the green grass of public lawns as the chill of winter lifts.

The daisy's Latin name comes from *bellis* for "pretty" and *perennis* for "everlasting." Its common name is thought to be derived from "day's eye," because the flower's petals close at night, which the nineteenth-century antiquarian and writer Thomas Wright noted in his *Specimens of Lyric Poetry*: "Dayes-eyes in this dales." Other common names include English daisy, bone flower, and woundwort, for its perceived healing capacity. There are many varieties of daisies, but all parts of the common daisy are edible. It should be noted that the flower is least bitter in bud form, and the buds can be pickled with salt, like capers (p. 56).

Image – p. 90

Hesperis matronalis

Dame's Rocket

Origin Eurasia
Type Forb
Blooms Early summer

Dame's rocket is a wildflower that goes by many names, including queen's gillyflower, damask violet, summer lilac, mother-of-the-evening, and dame's violet. The plant, as its various aliases imply, is a bit of a rogue lady. It sometimes passes for other purple-hued wildflowers—dame's rocket is often mistaken for wood phlox—and it becomes more fragrant as night falls, as is suggested by its genus name, *Hesperis*, from the Greek for "evening." To the Victorians, dame's rocket represented deceit as it concealed its scent during the day.

Dame's rocket is not often grown as a garden flower anymore and is most commonly considered a noxious weed. In fact, it's wanted by the authorities in four American states and in the Canadian province of Alberta, where restrictions have been placed on the dame's cultivation.

The whole plant is edible and its leaves have a peppery taste, similar to arugula (p. 28). The flower's flavor is best when it is still a bud, but its petals are edible as well. If you must pull dame's rocket from your garden, at least throw it into a salad.

Taraxacum officinale

Dandelion

Origin Eurasia
Type Forb
Blooms Year-round

Although today the dandelion is seen by many as an invader, popping its yellow head out of an expanse of otherwise manicured lawn, the flower has been present on the earth for millions of years: fossilized seeds of the dandelion's close relative, *Taraxacum tanaiticum*, found in Russia date to the Pliocene, some five million years ago, and the plant is thought to have existed tens of millions of years before that.

The humble dandelion has been a foodstuff for all of human history. It is thought by some to be one of the bitter herbs described in the Bible as being present at the Last Supper—and dandelion leaves can be eaten as *maror* during the Passover seder. It is also said that dandelion seeds were brought to America on the *Mayflower*. Today the dandelion can be found on six continents, but the varieties commercially cultivated for consumption are mainly native to Eurasia and North America.

The flower of the dandelion opens in the morning and closes at night or quickly after picking. Dandelion blossoms—unlike the bitter leaves—have a sweet, honeyed flavor. The entire plant—leaves, stems, flowers, and roots—is edible and nutritious. The buds and leaves may be cooked like spinach, and they also make an excellent salad when eaten raw. Italians are fond of dandelions and may have been the inventors of dandelion wine, made from the petals of the flower.

Hemerocallis fulva

Daylily

Origin Asia
Type Forb
Blooms Summer

The daylily is a precocious flower that burns brightly and quickly. It blooms for a single day: the daylily opens in the afternoon and remains through the night, and then is gone. Happily, it propagates easily, spilling over like a wildflower onto fields and roadsides, in crowds of bright orange swaying with the late summer breeze.

The daylily is not a true lily, which is important to note as many lilies are poisonous. Native to China and Japan, the daylily was likely brought to Europe by traders in the seventeenth century, and was then introduced to North America by European immigrants arriving in the late eighteenth century. Most commonly bright orange with a darker center, it also ranges from cream to pink to deep purple. A hardy perennial, it grows in patches and can stand up to three feet tall.

Early Chinese records list the daylily flower as a food source, as both the buds and petals can be eaten. They have a crunchy texture and a flavor reminiscent of snow peas, with a peppery aftertaste. Dried daylily buds, called *gum jum choi*, "golden needles," in Hong Kong, and *huang hua cai*, "yellow flower vegetable," in mainland China, are rehydrated and added to soups, noodle dishes, or other preparations as vegetables would be. Sliced daylily blooms can also be used in salads and soups. And, when the stamens and pistils are removed, the whole flower can be stuffed with cheese and breadcrumbs, coated with panko, and sautéed, similarly to a squash blossom (p. 203).

Images – pp. 95, 113

Daylily

Edible Flowers

Dill

Edible Flowers

Anethum graveolens

Dill

Origin Asia, northern Africa
Type Forb
Blooms Summer

Dill is a close relative of fennel (p. 105) and the two have strikingly similar wispy leaves and almost identical flowers. If you find yourself needing to identify the leaves and flowers of one from the other without the fennel's telltale bulb and stalks, smell proves the most effective guide, as dill emits a more pronounced citrus fragrance than fennel's mildly minty aroma. Dill flowers appear in flat umbels with bright yellow crowns on long, thin stems. Thought to be native to western Asia and northern Africa, the herb is perhaps today most commonly associated with Russian and Scandinavian cuisine, where it is infused into vodka, added to soups (a generous amount of dill can lift the earthy flavors of borscht), and used as an aromatic to steam or pickle fish. Its fine, feathery leaves can be plucked in larger sprigs or finely chopped and incorporated into dishes with seafood and yogurt. The herb is also featured in a soup for the Holy Ghost festival in Azores, Portugal. And, of course, dill is essential in the preparation of the most common American sandwich companion, the dill pickle. When making the brine, include the tiny flowers of blooming dill along with tender younger leaves.

Images — pp. 96, 110

Origanum dictamnus

Dittany

Origin Crete
Type Forb
Blooms Summer

Dittany is a flowering aromatic plant native to the Greek island of Crete. It has a sharp taste reminiscent of thyme (p. 209).

Dittany Tea
Evangelia Koutsovoulou with
Christina Kotsilelou

Like most recipes by Daphnis and Chloe, our brand of wild-grown Greek herbs, this one comes from a friend who happens to be a great cook. But this time we started with a question in mind: How can our herbs be used to make a refreshment that is special and essential? We wanted a recipe that would enhance the soft flavor of whole-leaf dried herbs. It had to be practical, easy to make, and, for us, sweetened with natural thyme honey, the best honey!

95 g thyme honey, or your preferred
    honey
zest of 1 organic unwaxed orange,
    plus two slices
4g dittany of Crete

To make a dittany and thyme honey syrup, into a small saucepan with ¾ cup water add the honey, orange slice, and zest. Bring the mixture to a boil. Remove from the heat and add the dittany. Steep for 10 minutes covered, then strain. Chill for 2 hours.

To serve, combine 1 part syrup with 2 parts sparkling water, add an orange slice to garnish, and serve over ice (or dittany-infused ice cubes).

Edible Flowers

Casting Nasturtiums

The first meal my dad made for my mum, back when she was a youthful twenty-two and he an astonishing and vaguely scandalous thirty-one, was some sort of souffléed omelet strewn with bright orange nasturtiums. He'd picked them himself. Essentially, he presented her with a plate of flowers, this was how he wooed her.

This meal, which has taken on the shine of legend, at least in the mind of its participants' daughter, came soon after my mother said to her friend, "The weirdo asked me out." The place was teacher training college, in the southeast London suburbs of the 1970s, and the weirdo was a bearded South African man who wore strange woolly sweaters, a man who'd left his homeland after he was told he might "accidentally" get shot if he continued his anti-apartheid activism. I wonder what it was like to go from a place of high southern hemisphere sun and biltong and wildebeests, to this cramped little place of drizzle and tea and squirrels.

He'd asked my mum on a date by writing her a note on a small sheet of paper, folding it into a paper airplane, and launching it from the library mezzanine to land on her desk below. I've never eaten a small paper airplane, but I imagine that, like a flower, it would crumple pleasingly between your teeth. A little note secreted about your person has the same sort of character as a flower popped into your mouth and swallowed—because I have in fact eaten nasturtium blooms and can report that they taste pleasingly peppery, as bright as their color. There is some illicit thrill to eating one of these blooms. A sense of haute-feminine decadence, for sure—let them eat flowers!—but also a current of brutality when you consider that something so beautiful, in all its delicate construction of veined orange silk and shivering stamens, can disappear in one bite.

I'm told that one of my best childhood malapropisms was asking if someone was "casting nasturtiums" on someone else's character. How much nicer to cast nasturtiums than aspersions—across omelets, across characters. I'm glad my mother ate her omelet and its flowers, cast no aspersions upon either it, or its creator. About a week later she decided she'd marry him.

Fuchsia found in El Masnou, a small village
near Barcelona.

Sambucus nigra

Elderflower

Origin Europe
Type Flowering shrub
Blooms Spring

"The Elder-Tree Mother," an 1845 fairy tale by Danish author Hans Christian Anderson, tells of a little boy who, while sick in bed, is given elderflower tea by his mother and soon sees visions—beginning with an elderberry tree growing from the teapot—as his kindly old neighbor spins a story. Though the elderflower's mild psychotropic properties will not inspire visions, it can be intoxicating: the flower is commonly associated today with the French liqueur St. Germain, a spirit that appeals to those with a taste for absinthe. The creamy, lacelike flowers are harvested by hand and distilled for their honeysuckle-peach flavor. Despite the Latin name of the elderberry, *Sambucus nigra*, the bush on which the elderflower blooms, the plant is not an ingredient of the anise-flavored liqueur.

The elderberry tree was a holy symbol of health in the Middle Ages, and its flowers were used in folk medicine and have long been associated with black magic. Even today, it can be found growing next to old houses in Great Britain as a protection against dark souls. "The common Elder, groweth everywhere," wrote the English botanist John Gerard in his *Herbal* of 1597, "That with jagged leaves growes in my garden." Elderflower appears in the folklore of countries including Germany, Denmark, Romania, Russia, and Scotland.

The flower of the elderberry tree—the elderflower—is edible. (The leaves, bark, and unripe green berries are toxic. It should also be noted that the red berries of other species of the *Sambucus* genus are poisonous and should never be confused.) The small white blossoms are highly fragrant and sweet when added to tea blends or used to make floral water. Elderflower cordials are a common preparation, but the flowers can also be incorporated into cooking in a variety of ways, including lightly battering and frying them to make lacy fritters, or *hollerküchel*, as they're known in Germany and Austria.

Images — pp. 103, 112

Elderflower

Edible Flowers

Fennel

Edible Flowers

Foeniculum vulgare

Fennel

Origin Eurasia
Type Forb
Blooms Summer, fall

Fennel, a humble herbaceous perennial, may once have lent its name to a city. Across ancient Greece, the fennel plant—*marathon*—was so plentiful that the town south of Athens was named after it.

Fennel is a member of the Apiaceae family, which makes it a cousin to carrot and celery. The fennel's tiny blossoms appear in constellation-like clusters—like bright yellow fireworks—at the end of thin stems that shoot from a large white bulb and look strikingly similar to dill flowers (p. 97). The blooms each hold pollen, which makes fennel attractive to butterflies. If left to its own devices, fennel will self-sow.

Native to the Eurasia, fennel is now enjoyed around the world. The seeds, bulb, and stalks have a sweet anise or licorice flavor that is milder in the feathery leaves and small flowers. Fennel pollen, which has become as alluring to people as it is to butterflies, has a stronger, honeyed taste that sets it apart.

Fennel blossoms can add flavor and color to a variety of preparations, from salads and soups, to pickle mixes and fresh pastas, to cookies and muffins. The flowers are also a natural addition to recipes that call for fennel bulbs, such as sausages or fish dishes. Sprinkle a pinch of fennel pollen on savory dishes to give them a lift.

Images — pp. 104, 117, 215

Tanacetum parthenium

Feverfew

Origin Eurasia
Type Forb
Blooms Summer

Feverfew is a relative of chamomile; small and daisylike in appearance, it also has white petals that fan around a central yellow core. The plant's common name derives from the Latin word *febrifugia*, which translates as "fever reducer." True to its moniker, the plant has long been thought to have medicinal properties and the flower is still acknowledged as a treatment for headaches, specifically migraines. The whole plant is edible, but the flowers have a bitter taste that can counter sweeter flavors in a fruit salad or compote.

Image – p. 111

Myosotis spp.

Forget-Me-Not

Origin Eurasia
Type Forb
Blooms Spring

Forget-me-not's genus name, *Myosotis*, comes from the Ancient Greek word for "mouse's ear," which the leaves of the plants in this genus were thought to resemble. The periwinkle-blue flower of the *Myosotis sylvatica* blooms in temperate climates in spring and its blossoms are tiny and numerous, seemingly the inspiration behind ditsy floral patterns. Its common name, forget-me-not, implies its long symbolic history as a humble plea of remembrance, as if in sweet supplication, "please, remember me." The flower has been adopted as an insignia by organizations fighting Alzheimer's disease, and as a symbol commemorating the Armenian genocide.

The flowers are the only edible part of the forget-me-not, and can be used as decorative elements on cakes and sweets, added to salads, or, as Leif Hedendal demonstrates in his recipe on page 243, used to garnish vegetable dishes.

Images – pp. 4, 115

Edible Flowers

Forsythia spp.

Forsythia

Origin Eurasia
Type Flowering shrub
Blooms Spring

Forsythia blooms in spring, lighting up branches that sit bare all winter with vivid yellow star-shaped flowers for only a few weeks. During this brief period, its peak bloom typically coincides with Easter, which is why the shrub is sometimes called Easter tree. Forsythia is native to Eurasia and is considered one of the primary herbs in Chinese herbology. The flowers have a mild floral taste and are best eaten raw.

Image – p. 114

Fuchsia spp.

Fuchsia

Origin South America
Type Flowering shrub
Blooms Early spring

Fuchsia is the type of flower that everyone can unite around, the kind that inspires flower enthusiasts to form societies dedicated to the beauty of its blooms—like the American Fuchsia Society, established in 1929. It's not that fuchsia is the only flower to elicit such enthusiasm, but it is arguably one of the most deserving, as the unearthly fuchsia is a bloom to behold. Though species of fuchsia vary slightly in appearance, all hang off the vine like a decorative lantern or pendant. Typically bright pink and purple, each tubular flower opens into an umbrella-like shade to reveal more layers of ruffled petals from which emerge long, tassel-like stamens and a large stigma. Fuchsia was first collected by Europeans in the Dominican Republic in the late 1600s, but was named after the German botanist Leonhart Fuchs, who had lived more than a century before.

Fuchsia grows best in tropical climates, and the dazzling appearance of its flowers attracts hummingbirds. Fuchsia plants produce berries that resemble elongated cherries and have a kiwi-like taste, and the flowers are edible as well, with a subtle and pleasant tartness.

Image – p. 101

Edible Flowers

Allium spp.

Garlic, Onion

Origin Pan-global
Type Forb
Blooms Summer

Of the hundreds of species of the genus *Allium*, the most familiar include kitchen staples such as onions, chives, ramps, shallots, and garlic. All are edible and all flower. Though they vary in shape, flavor, and size, the basic structure of all alliums remains the same: the bulb of the plant is underground and its stems shoot up in scapes that burst open with a spherical inflorescence. The individual flowers range from white to pale violet to purple and are tiny and star-shaped with a beaded center. Some varieties have densely packed, bushy florets. Others, such as drumstick allium, are more solid and compact, almost like a pincushion.

Evidence of the cultivation of garlic has been found on cuneiform records from over five thousand years ago. It is believed that ancient Egyptian royals fed garlic to the workers who built the pyramids to give them strength, and garlic was found in the tomb of King Tutankhamen. It was perhaps the ancient Greeks and Romans who attributed to garlic its supernatural properties, instilling garlic into religious and magical rituals, including the ideas that garlic can repel scorpions and protect against the spread of illness if placed above the entrance to a house, a precursor perhaps to the later belief in garlic's power to ward off vampires.

Native peoples of the Americas made a tea from allium bulbs to treat illness. Portuguese explorers brought the contemporary cultivar we know as garlic today, and later, in nineteenth-century America, Shakers listed garlic in their herb catalogues as a stimulant.

Allium blossoms are edible (although ornamental alliums should not be eaten, as they have likely been sprayed with pesticides) and produce a taste comparable to the vegetable part of the plant, but milder. The flowers can be baked into breads, used in soups, pickled, sautéed, and applied as a garnish on any dish that garlic or onion would suit.

Images — pp. 82, 109

Dill

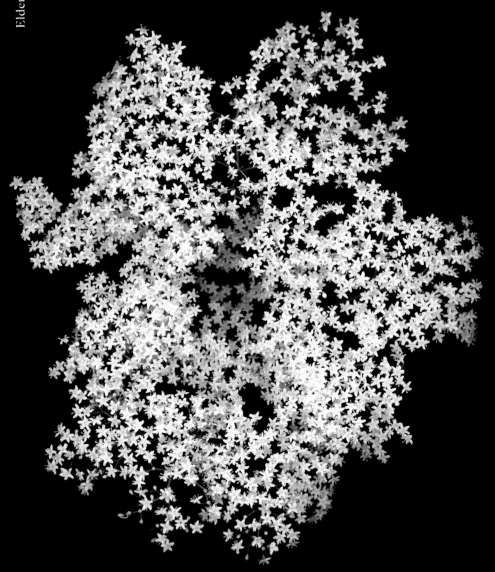

Forsythia

Gladiolus

Gladiolus spp.

Gladiolus

Origin Africa
Type Forb
Blooms Summer

With its blade-shaped leaves, it's no surprise that gladiolus takes its name from the Latin *gladius*, meaning "sword." Another common name for it is sword lily, which is as literal a description as one could hope for. Gladiolus flowers cluster on one side of tall stems that grow upwards of three feet tall and emulate a spike. The blossoms are funnel-shaped with ruffled edges and look papery and delicate, despite the plant's assertive name and demeanor.

The flower has long been associated with triumph and success in athleticism, as gladioli are thought to have been thrown at the feet of victorious Roman gladiators—indeed *gladiator* shares an etymon with *gladiolus*. The Dutch phrase "death or the gladioli" meaning "do or die," sometimes credited to cycling champion Gerrie Knetemann, sums up the competitor's two options: to be feted with flowers or killed by the opponent. The victory gladiolus prevails today at a four-day recreational march held each year in Nijmegen, in the Netherlands, where the flower is presented to each person as they cross the finish on a street temporarily renamed Via Gladiola.

Native to South Africa, the gladiolus was brought to Holland in the eighteenth century, and many of the hundreds of hybrids known today were cultivated during this period. The flower can be stuffed like a daylily (p. 94), and its petals have a crisp, lettuce-like quality.

Image – p. 120

Solidago spp.

Goldenrod

Origin North America
Type Forb
Blooms Summer, fall

Roadsides erupting in gold, signaling the end of summer, are often how Europeans and Americans experience the blossoming of goldenrod. The plant was brought west from the Middle East in the sixteenth century as a cure-all, its Latin name *Solidago* meaning "to make whole."

In North America, the plant has figured notably in two episodes in history, first as an ingredient in liberty tea, a black tea substitute drunk by the patriots following the Boston Tea Party in 1773, when tea was suddenly in short supply. Second, in the 1920s, when Thomas Edison looked to the plant to assist him with another shortage, this time in tires: "Packed in his five carloads of laboratory material were tons of stalks of a common, ubiquitous weed: goldenrod. Goldenrod... seemed a likely US weed from which to produce the object of his major research in the past two years: Rubber," reported *Time* in 1929. An adequate substitute for rubber could ultimately not be extracted from the plant, but in the collection of Edison's research records at the New York Botanical Garden's LuEsther T. Mertz Library, *Solidago* alone occupies more than five hundred shelves.

All of the goldenrod is edible and its flavor is similar to anise, with a bitter and minty taste. Throw goldenrod flowers on a salad, use them as an aromatic, or get really clever and invent something new.

Image — p. 123

Goldenrod

Edible Flowers

Hibiscus

124

Edible Flowers

Hibiscus rosa-sinesis

Hibiscus

Origin Asia
Type Flowering shrub
Blooms Summer

Hibiscus is the platonic tropical flower; its familiar large trumpet-shaped, crepe-like petals in bright reds and pinks, and pistil that shoots up from the center are easy to call to mind. The origin of the hibiscus is uncertain, but it is the national flower of Malaysia and is found, and consumed, in many tropical climates.

The flower and calyx (the pod from which the flower emerges) can be eaten cooked or raw. Hibiscus is used as a dye and a mild spice for its tart flavor. A tea high in vitamin C is brewed from hibiscus blossoms in many parts of the world. In Egypt, hibiscus tea is known as *karkadé*. In Cambodia, the flowers are steeped in hot water until the color seeps out and lime is added. And in Jamaica, hibiscus tea is drunk with a dash of rum. In Mexico, a refreshingly tart *agua fresca* made with concentrate from the dried flowers—*agua de Jamaica*—sometimes includes cinnamon. Dried hibiscus is also used in Mexican desserts, including chocolate produced in Oaxaca City.

Images – pp. 118, 124

Alcea rosea

Hollyhock

Origin Asia
Type Forb
Blooms Summer

The elegant hollyhock, which grows on tall stems that spiral upward, lends itself well to stylization and artistic interpretation. The Hollyhock House was designed by Frank Lloyd Wright in 1919 for the oil heiress Aline Barnsdall and named for her favorite flower, which was featured in the garden and used as a decorative motif throughout the residence. The hollyhock also figures prominently in many of Georgia O'Keeffe's paintings including *Ram's Head, White Hollyhock-Hills* of 1935. Indeed, hollyhock is the official flower of Taos, New Mexico, in the same region as the O'Keeffe homestead in Abiquiú. The hollyhock is native to China and was introduced to Britain in 1573. From there it spread globally. The whole hollyhock is edible and the petals can be thrown into salads or steeped to make tea.

Image – p. 119

Lonicera spp.

Honeysuckle

Origin Pan-global
Type Flowering shrub
Blooms Summer

One might imagine that honeysuckle represents what all nectar tastes like: ambrosia seeping from the core of a blossom. Honeysuckle thrives throughout summer, attracting bees, butterflies, birds, and children exploring their backyards. The highly familiar Japanese variety grows wild on a vine with thin, two-inch, trumpetlike orange and white flowers. Suffused into a simple syrup, honeysuckle can flavor a range of summery treats. In the American South, where the scent of the flower hangs in the humid air, honeysuckle is whipped into butter and sometimes adorns Hummingbird Cake, a beloved and oft-adapted recipe that achieves its airy sweetness through the addition of canned pineapple and banana.

Image – p. 116

Humulus lupulus

Hops

Origin Eurasia
Type Flowering vine
Blooms Summer

Due to the popularization of craft beer, most people are familiar with the taste of hops. Hops are the flowering part of the common hop plant. They look like tiny bright green pine cones and have a natural antimicrobial essence that allows them to ferment with less spoilage, making them a crucial element of beer brewing. Though slightly younger in recorded history than other bitter herbs like dandelion (p. 93) or marigold (p. 144), early records show that a hop garden was left to the Roman emperor Charlemagne by his father Pepin the Short. Monks are generally credited with discovering the benefits of hops in fermentation, and Holland was first to export ales created with hops to England in the Middle Ages, though England became the largest producer of the flowers in the nineteenth century.

The hops plant grows in vines and is trained to climb trellises; from a distance, a field of hops might look like a vineyard. Harvesting hops is a labor-intensive process and from the mid-1800s through the 1950s, Londoners wanting an escape to the countryside migrated seasonally to the hop fields. At the height of hops picking some forty thousand people, often families, traveled to Kent for three weeks in September. The harvest was advertised as "a sociable out-of-door occupation combined with the pleasures of a lengthy and enjoyable picnic" by the *Illustrated Sporting and Dramatic News* in 1943, which expanded on the ways in which the harvesting conditions had vastly improved since the Victorian era, when living quarters were "primitive." This appealing coverage was likely meant to draw women to the fields during World War II, when they made up the majority of the harvest labor. Hops picking is well documented in photographs and explored in English writer Somerset Maugham's 1915 novel *Of Human Bondage*, which culminates with his protagonist Philip Carey falling in love with young Sally as they accompany her family to a hops harvest.

Hops are best when fermented, but can also be used like a bay leaf. See Tara Thomas's recipe for Hopping Clover Kombucha on page 235.

Giant hyssop growing at Longwood Gardens, Pennsylvania.

Agastache foeniculum

Hyssop

Origin North America
Type Forb
Blooms Summer, early fall

Hyssop is both a visual and culinary treat. Its bottle-brush-like spears of violet flowers pop up around the end of summer and persist into fall. It is slightly bitter, with a strong fresh and floral flavor and fragrance, derived from its heritage in the mint family. The flowering herb, which adds a burst of purple to the garden, is also extremely easy to grow and harvest throughout summer. In cooking and baking, its flowers and leaves can be a flavorful and unexpected addition. Add finely chopped hyssop flowers to dough when making shortbread, or cook it as you would rosemary or mint with beef, lamb, or pork.

Image – p. 128

Castilleja spp.

Indian Paintbrush

Origin North America
Type Forb
Blooms Summer

Indian paintbrush, also known as castilleja and prairie fire, looks just like its common names suggest—blazing and brushlike. The plant is native to western North America, where it stands out from desert land-scapes in swaths of intense persimmon-red. Indian paintbrush flowers are fully edible, have a honeyed taste, and have long been a foodstuff to native peoples. See Gina Rae La Cerva's essay on Indian paintbrush on page 133.

Image – p. 135

Edible Flowers

Jasminum sambac

Jasmine

Origin Asia
Type Flowering vine
Blooms Summer, fall

Only *Jasminum sambac*, or Arabian jasmine, is edible. All other species of jasmine are poisonous, although their strongly perfumed flower looks similar between varieties, which makes accurate identification especially important. Jasmine is native to Southeast Asia and common in the Philippines, where *Jasminum sambac* is the national flower; in Indonesia, where it is incorporated into wedding ceremonies as garlands; and in Hawaii, where it is one of the flowers commonly made into leis. Jasmine often scents green tea and it can be fermented or made into a floral syrup.

Image – p. 146

Pueraria montana

Kudzu

Origin Asia
Type Flowering vine
Blooms Summer

Kudzu is sometimes called "the vine that ate the South" as it covers large expanses of woods, killing other plants and even trees, and creeps up the Georgian brick houses of the southern United States. Native to Asia, it was first brought to North American for the Japanese exhibit at the 1876 Centennial Exposition in Philadelphia and promoted as a means of controlling erosion. Once introduced into gardens, it quickly grew out of control, as it remains today. Its flowers are a rare sight and smell—bright purple with an almost unnaturally sweet grape scent. The plant is in the pea family, and its blossoms are similarly shaped, but appear in a more extravagant cluster almost resembling wisteria blossoms growing upward. Everything but the vine is edible, and kudzu flowers can be made into jelly, wine, or sorbet, or stir-fried with collard greens.

Lavendula spp.

Lavender

Origin Mediterranean
Type Forb
Blooms Summer

Lavender immediately conjures linen sachets and perfumed soaps. Its scent, which evokes both rosemary and sage with a strong floral edge, can overtake a room. In fact, it has been prized for centuries for its cleansing fragrance, which is how it earned its name: lavender derives from the Latin *lavare*, "to wash."

The earliest known use of lavender is in baths in ancient Greece, where it was thought to purify the body, and the New Testament of the Bible cites two instances when Jesus is anointed with lavender oil. Though cultivation of the herb declined with the fall of the Roman Empire, it remained growing in monastery gardens in the Middle Ages and was eventually introduced to sixteenth-century England, where it was used to freshen clothing, to repel insects, and as a treatment for migraines. Queen Elizabeth I reportedly demanded fresh lavender flowers for her rooms and drank ten cups of tea brewed with the flower every day. It was often used as a savory rub for meats, and later, it was crushed into castor sugar to infuse cakes and other sweets. During the Victorian era, when advances in dye technology led to a fashion for purples of all varieties, lavender was also beloved. The Provence region of France is known for its lavender fields, which bloom in stunning expanses of dusky purple from June to mid-July.

As an edible flower, lavender can brighten berries, balancing their sweetness, or add a perfumed layer to meats and cheeses. Lavender is also often added to shortbread. A little lavender goes a long way, so use it sparingly.

Image – p. 147

Edible Flowers

Glycyrrhiza glabra

Licorice

Origin Eurasia, North Africa
Type Forb
Blooms Summer

Licorice has a deep, earthy, sweet smell and a flavor that is polarizing: its stridently fennel and anise taste can require a mature palate. Its slightly smoky quality—like scotch or mezcal—has also made it a common additive in tobacco and snuff.

   The dried sticks of licorice root were once sold as chewable sweets in the Netherlands, where licorice-flavored candy remains a popular treat today. While licorice candy now includes less of the plant than it used to—anise extract is commonly added to boost the distinctive flavor—it contains enough *Glycyrrhiza glabra* to cause harm if too much is ingested: in 2019, an American man died after eating a bag or two of black licorice every day for three weeks. But fear not. As with other edible flowers, consumption in moderation is safe.

   Glycyrrhiza glabra looks similar to hyssop (p. 129), but with small cylindrical purple blossoms. Licorice flowers can be added to salads or brewed as a tea, infused into sugar, or baked into sweets such as shortbread cookies.

Indian Paintbrush

Indian paintbrush (castilleja), also known as painted cup, painted lady, grandmother's hair, butterfly weed, prairie fire.

This wildflower has entranced me since childhood. The spiky crimson-red clusters burst out of the hot, dry desert soil and rock crevices like little gifts. I would kneel in the dust and pick the little tubes protruding from the top of the plant, bright green at the tip and hidden white within. Pull gently and they pop out. Suck the tips delicately and a sweet nectar blasts the tongue. An excellent wet flourish on a hot day spent exploring.

Red flowers are rare because many insects do not detect the color. So these flowers are pollinated by butterflies, bees, and hummingbirds. These creatures don't need to perch, but hover over the flower and lick down the long tubes to find the hidden sweetness. Of the two hundred species of Indian paintbrush found across the United States, New Mexico has eleven. I'm not sure which variety I so loved as a kid.

But only with time have I learned the Indian paintbrush's secrets. This plant is a deception. The scarlet petals are in fact modified leaves called bracts. The flower is inconspicuous, merely the small lateral lobes I would pick, formed by petals curling and wrapping around each other.

These plants are hemiparasitic: while they can perform photosynthesis, most often this process does not provide enough nutrients on its own for them to survive. Castilleja look to other vegetation for sustenance by sending out specialized roots called haustoria, which reach through the soil until they touch the roots of another plant. A sagebrush or chamisa bush perhaps. And then these Indian paintbrush carefully penetrate the root tissues of this other being and thieve their food and water. The host plants may not thrive as well as they would have without the parasitic flower, but perhaps they are content in knowing they have increased the biodiversity of the region by sharing with these vivid blooms.

Indian paintbrush is a flower that should be consumed in moderation. Horses have died from eating too many. The plants accumulate selenium from the soil. In small amounts, it can be used medicinally to help aid menstrual cycles and ease aching joints, turned into a wash to make hair glossy or to use as a red dye, or employed as a love charm. In large amounts, it is a poison.

My childhood is a flash through my mind of riotous sweetness, flaming edible wildflowers emerging from the parched soil. My childhood was parasitic, dependent on the high mountain deserts where I lived and the bold Indian paintbrush that bloomed in spring and stayed vibrant all summer. As a child, I understood each flower to be an individual. I thought of them as friends. Were they artists, as their name implies? I almost could intuit the strange fact that we share a quarter of our genes with these plants. They grow from seed one year, live another to blossom and shed their own seeds to the wind, and then they are gone, a life of brief brilliance.

Indian paintbrush wild in Abiquiú, New Mexico

Syringa vulgaris

Lilac

Origin Europe
Type Flowering shrub
Blooms Spring

There are two heirloom lilac shrubs brought to the United States from Europe in the 1700s that still bloom. One is planted at Thomas Jefferson's plantation, Monticello, in Virginia. The other is on Laura Ingalls Wilder's homestead in Malone, New York. These enduring shrubs seem to embody the best of the lilac: loyal and hardy once it gets settled. It can take a few years for a lilac to acclimate enough to bloom, and once it does, the fragrant flowers last only a few weeks in spring. But the shrubs are long-lived and can be passed down through generations.

Lilacs bloom in soft conical clusters densely populated with small heart-shaped blossoms that are most commonly a pale pinkish-purple or white. The scent of lilac—an irresistible pleasure of spring—is much stronger than its taste, which is slightly citrusy, though the flavor can vary from plant to plant. It is best to steep or soak the blossoms to bring out the flavor of the flower, as lilac—as has been established—likes to take its time.

Images — pp. 150, 151

Nelumbo spp.

Lotus

Origin Asia, North America
Type Forb
Blooms Summer

The lotus flower is often depicted as the pillow-like floating seat of the Buddha. Its blossom, when fully open, glows with an otherworldly presence as if calling you to submit, to meditate, to be present in the moment that the lotus is occupying. How the lotus came to represent the philosophical idea of being is rooted in Eastern religions and the natural growing patterns of the flower, which emerges from murky water and prevails, blossoming poetically, as if it is hovering above the rest of the world's troubles.

(Lotus, cont.)

Homer brought the lotus into focus in his epic poem *The Odyssey*: "On the tenth day we reached the land of the Lotus-eaters, who live on a food that comes from a kind of flower." Lotus eaters, as he described them, are listless souls lingering eternally over what is in front of them—in contrast to the conquering spirit of the hero, Odysseus. James Joyce subtly evokes the spirit of this passage in the fifth narrative episode of *Ulysses*, often dubbed "Lotus Eaters," which depicts a lifeless urban street scene. The "lotus eater" has remained an archetype of sleepy apathy, likened to people who lay low in larger societal structures, lacking the inner fight of ambition, for better or worse. Though lotus is not presently in fashion as a plant medicine, its more modern counterparts (psilocybin or ayahuasca) are sought for similar effects when one wishes to quiet the ego.

Though it is said that the Greek word *lôtos*, which Homer used in his poem, could also have referred to nettle (p. 163) or water lily (p. 214), a blue lotus was cultivated by the Egyptians, and is recorded as having both soporific and psychotropic qualities. The Ebers Papyrus, an Egyptian medical document dating to around 1550 BCE, notes the harvesting of water lily and lotus flowers as food for both the living and the dead, and lotus is listed as an offering to kings in the afterlife, so they could, one assumes, rest easy.

All parts of the lotus plant are edible and it is a common ingredient in Chinese cuisine. Its thick root is most ubiquitous and often steamed, but the holes of the sliced root can also be stuffed with preserved fruit, meat, or glutinous rice. The whole lotus blossom, after the stamen and sepals are removed, is edible and can be battered and fried. The lotus is also made into a jelly that is popular around the New Year as a symbol of hope for sweet months ahead.

Edible Flowers

Magnolia spp.

Magnolia

Origin North America
Type Flowering tree
Blooms Spring

The magnolia is most closely associated with the hot and humid southern United States—it is the official flower of both Mississippi and Louisiana—where the shade offered by the tree is well appreciated. Across this territory, two varieties are most common: the southern magnolia (*Magnolia grandiflora*) and the saucer magnolia (*Magnolia × soulangeana*), both of which blossom in spring. The southern magnolia is an imposing tree with rubbery, deep green leaves and large, creamy white flowers, while the saucer magnolia is smaller and erupts with pale pink blossoms.

The ancient magnolia has been planted around the world since the 1700s, but it is native to and one of the oldest trees in the United States. The southern magnolia has become a poignant emblem of the dichotomies of the American South—its stately apprearance is often romaticized, but it also appears as a more haunting symbol in the Abel Meeropol poem "Strange Fruit." The tree is an apt reminder of history and perseverance, as it is thousands of years old and has prevailed through floods and fires, as the bark of the tree is fire resistant and its roots are strong enough to weather the intense storms of this region.

The white flowers of the southern magnolia are edible, though eating them raw is not encouraged. The petals are best pickled and preserved, and their sour-sweet flavor endures the treatment. The flowers, which bloom in May and June, are very fragrant and attract pollinators with their sweet secretions. The saucer magnolia's buds can be picked and pickled, to be used in Japanese cuisine similarly to *gari*, pickled ginger.

Images — pp. 139, 148, 153

Saucer magnolia

Edible Flowers

Okra flower

Edible Flowers

Okra Flower

I told myself that one day I'd grow the food that raised me. When I knew well enough how to grow, that I'd take what I'd learnt and grow the food of my family. This year was the first in a garden of my own, after a number of seasons growing crops on land that belonged to someone else. In this garden, I dared to grow plants that would declare that the soil was mine to tend.

The first time I sowed okra seeds, it was later than it ought to have been and it took three tries before they agreed to germinate. When the suggestion of a sprout crested the compost, neck first, it was even later still. Nonetheless I watched with anticipation, in hope, that they'd grow, maybe catch up, in the heat that was gathering as spring gave way to summer. Two little seed leaves, like a clam shell, emerged and fell open with the promise of palmate leaves and flowers akin to hibiscus cousins and firm tapered pods to come.

I'd heard of how okra seeds were braided into the hair of those stolen across the Atlantic to be enslaved. How that's how the food of our ancestors came to be in the Americas. I often wonder if that's how okra made its way to Mauritius too, though I've yet to find or hear a story that tells me so. Such is the way of colonial erasure. These sacred plants will root into English soil this year, as I—a foreigner too—have tried to for thirty-six turns around the sun.

The growth was, at first, somewhat sedate among the three seedlings that survived an unceremonious battering by a young hen's foraging claws. The leaves unfurled, one after another, nevertheless, dotted with tiny beads of sap that hardened into crystal balls, until the first flower bloomed in early August.

It appeared, all cream crepe petals with burgundy wine at the center, and within a day had retreated, withering to make way for the pod that would swell in its place. I'd only ever eaten the fruit, but the leaves and the flowers are edible too. I didn't dare eat the first few blooms; I wanted the pods that were the food of my childhood. I was fussy when young, but not when it came to okra, lady's-fingers, l'aloo-spiced and slightly singed at the corners, cooked with tomatoes sometimes. It was never the slimy disaster that it's so often accused of being when a Mauritian watches over the pot.

I was determined to try a flower enough that I surrendered into forsaking a precious pod to find out what I was missing. I checked every day, under the leaves like outstretched palms, searching for a pointed bud on the verge of cresting, and poised myself to pick it in time. It felt like sacrilege to interrupt the cycle midway, but I stayed hopeful while I harvested this treasure.

I laid the delicate trumpet, worshipfully, on a board and carefully dissected it before placing it on my tongue. Eyes closed, breath gently held, I put a segment of petal, stamen, and stigma into mouth and let it rest there in anticipation of a riot of flavor. There was so little to taste that I worried I was doing it wrong. A tiny sweetness, a trace of pepper, but all in all, more texture than taste. Not quite worthy of the sacrifice.

And so, with taste buds unignited, underwhelmed, I thought about the pod that would never be, in the year of sowing too late, in a climate too cool for flourishing. Next year, if they grace me with their presence, I'll leave them be. I'll leave the flowers to the bees, and the pods, however few, I will gather for my family and me.

Madhuca longifolia

Mahua

Origin Asia
Type Flowering tree
Blooms Spring

The intensely sweet, pale yellow flowers of the mahua tree support entire ecosystems of humans and animals in central India in summer, when crops can fail because of drought. It is the food of survival, and people have found innumerable ways to transform every part of the mahua's offerings—flowers, fruits, seeds, and leaves—into necessities such as flour, cooking oil, *sabzis* (Indian vegetable dishes), and cattle fodder. But the bulbous flowers are most beloved when fermented and made into a potent liquor—the only one made of sweet flowers in the world. Read Sneha Mehta's essay on mahua on page 87.

Malva spp.

Mallow

Origin Europe, Africa
Type Forb
Blooms Summer

The mallow family, aka Malvaceae, is a large family of flowers that also includes hollyhock (p. 126) and hibiscus (p. 125). The flowers of these plants are similar, with papery petals that have ornamental markings that vary from thin stripes to variegated colors. The root of one species of mallow is thought to be an original ingredient in the fluffy, sugary treat, the marshmallow. Mallow flowers, native to Africa and Europe, were exploited for their high nutritional value for more than two thousand years and were cultivated by Romans to stuff suckling pigs. The seeds of the common mallow, *Malva neglecta*, are high in protein, and its leaves contain calcium, potassium, and vitamins A and C. Like okra (p. 164), mallow leaves are mucilaginous and can be used to thicken soups, or eaten like spinach, cooked or raw.

Images – pp. 74, 149

Tagetes spp.

Marigold

Origin South America, tropical America
Type Forb
Blooms Summer, fall

Marigolds are best in abundance. The ruffled orange globes crowd together naturally, overtaking entire fields and causing the earth to overflow with color. Millions of blooms cozy up in teeming mounds at markets, and adorn alters and drench the roads for the Day of the Dead in Mexico.

Marigolds are native to the Americas and were valued by the Aztecs for both their medicinal and magical properties. In the fifteenth and sixteenth centuries, the flowers were disseminated via what is now known as the Columbian Exchange, the flow of both goods and ideas from the so-called New World to the Old World. Along with bougainvillea (p. 49), potato, and chili, the marigold made its way to India, China, and Europe and rapidly assimilated into the cultures of each region, especially India, where the marigold features prominently in the festival of Diwali and has been integrated into Ayurvedic practice. *Tagetes erecta* earned another of its common names, African marigold, as it came to England via North Africa (the French marigold, *Tagetes patula*, a smaller species, arrived in England from France.)

Marigolds are edible and dynamic when incorporated into cooking— they complement both sweet and savory flavors, and they can be eaten raw or blanched. Their yellow coloring has been used as a less costly substitute for saffron (p. 198). Dairy women in England once churned the petals of the marigold with their cream to lend their butter a deeper color. Try pressing marigold petals on butter for a beautiful display.

Images – pp. 69, 145, 155

Mentha spp.

Mint

Origin Pan-global
Type Forb
Blooms Summer

Mint is best regarded in the plural—mints—as the herbs of the mint family, Lamiaceae, are both widespread and numerous. Mints are perhaps native to the Mediterranean region, but there are few places on earth where they do not grow today. Gardeners experience the rapid proliferation of the herb soon after it is planted, but mints are also wild, found as weeds in any moist and partly sunny areas. The most common of the mint genus, *Mentha*, are spearmint (*Mentha spicata*) and the horticultural hybrid peppermint (*Mentha × piperita*), and the word "mint" has long been accepted as a colloquial name for any sugary, minty-flavored candy.

Fossilized mint seeds suggest the plant dates back millions of years, and mints are mentioned in every herbalist text from Pliny's *Natural History* to English botanist John Gerard's *Herball*, which both cite the vast medicinal uses of the herb. (Of mint, Gerard wrote it is "marvelous wholesome for the stomach.") Mints are deeply fragrant and their applications as extensive as their history. The flavor and scent of all mints is strong, effervescent, and cleansing, and the experience of eating it can be transportive, like cool water rushing over your senses. This quality has been remarked on for centuries and articulated nicely by the English physician Tobias Venner, who wrote in his 1620 *A Plaine Philosophical Discourse on Nature* that mints "greatly comfort the braine and spirits, stirre up the senses, especially the memorie, and make the heart cheerefull."

Mints are fully edible, including their green pointed leaves and flowers, which shoot up in small purple cylinders. In cooking, the uses of mints are also endless as there are few flavors they don't elevate. Mint flowers, like all flowering herbs, can be used in the same ways as the leafy greens. Mints are used to make Moroccan Touareg tea, candy and sweets, jellies to accompany savory dishes like lamb and curries in India, and classic cocktails such as mint juleps or mojitos.

Sinapis alba

Mustard

Origin Mediterannean, Middle East
Type Forb
Blooms Spring

The seeds of white mustard, *Sinapis alba*, are ground and mixed with vinegar, water, salt, and turmeric to produce the common yellow table mustard squeezed onto hot dogs at ballparks, though other varieties of mustard plant are enlisted to prepare different types of the condiment— Dijon, for example, is made from ground brown mustard (*Brassica juncea*). While the plant is usually grown for its seeds, the flowers also have many uses. Whole mustard flowers can be used like a fresh herb as an aromatic (though the tiny flowers disappear when heated). They can also be tossed into salads or used as garnish.

The whole mustard plant is also useful in gardens as it keeps soil aerated. In California's Napa Valley, the plant is grown among vineyards for this purpose. When the grapevines are dormant, it is common to see sunny fields of yellow mustard flowers.

Image – p. 154

Tropaeolum majus

Nasturtium

Origin South America
Type Forb
Blooms Summer

A mainstay of cottage and herb gardens, the nasturtium has prevailed throughout history. The flower's brightly hued, trumpet-shaped blooms speckle Claude Monet's central path at Giverny and make their way into avant-gardist Alice B. Toklas's famed 1954 cookbook as a key ingredient in her 14th of July Salad (a concoction of mayonnaise, capers, pickles, cucumbers, and whitefish). For centuries, nasturtium's versatility has lent it well to myriad uses. The flowers, leaves, buds, pods, and seeds of the nasturtium plant are edible and have a strong, spicy bite similar to watercress. They also provide a colorful addition to salads, pasta, and egg dishes. The stems and leaves can be blended with olive oil, garlic, pine nuts, and Pecorino or Parmesan cheeses to make a pesto.

While nasturtium is known for its distinct peppery taste, its sharp, pungent odor inspired its name: *nasus*, "a nose," and *tortus*, "twisted." Spanish botanist Nicolás Monardes first brought the flower, which likely originates in Bolivia and Peru, to Europe in 1569. Its genus name, *Tropaeolum*, derived from the Greek word meaning "trophy," can be credited to Swedish naturalist Carolus Linnaeus. The rounded leaves and blooms, he observed, bore a resemblance to the shields and helmets that soldiers once seized as trophies on the battlefield. Nasturtium is also commonly called monk's cress for its funnel-shaped blossoms that call to mind a monk's hood.

The American arts patron and collector Isabella Stewart Gardner featured the flower prominently at her Boston museum in the annual display Hanging Nasturtiums. Every April, the orange blossoms spill over the balconies of the museum's Venetian-style courtyard in honor of Gardner's birthday and the advent of spring. Though the installation lasts only a few weeks, the flowers are nurtured year-round: the nasturtium is sown in the summer months and cultivated in the Gardner

(cont.)

(Nasturtium, cont.)

Museum's greenhouses throughout the winter. The museum's café has been known to highlight the jewel-toned flower on its menu.

The long trailing vines of nasturtium have been growing wild since ancient times. There are many different varieties that can be found in climbing, semitrailing, and dwarf forms. The plant's easy-to-grow nature has made it popular among amateur and professional gardeners alike, including Thomas Jefferson, who documented the planting of nasturtium "in the meadow" of Monticello. It is said that he frequently used the buds and seeds to garnish his salads.

Image — p. 182

Thelesperma megapotanicum

Navajo Tea

Origin Mexico, North America
Type Forb
Blooms Summer

Indigenous to the American Southwest, Navajo tea, also called greenthread, is a relative of the sunflower (p. 207) and daisy (p. 91). Often brewed as a tea, its flavor is grassy and cooling.

Navajo Tea
Andi Murphy

Navajo tea also goes by Indian tea or greenthread. It is a long and thin plant that sprouts small yellow flowers in June and July. When the flowers barely start to bloom, that's the time to harvest. The harvested plants are bundled up and dried and saved to make hot tea and iced tea. The tea has one of the best aromas: like rain in the desert. If these plants grow near you, feel free to harvest them. If they don't grow in your area, there are a few Indigenous food companies out there that could have some for purchase.

bundle of dried Navajo tea
sweetener of your choice, such as
    honey or agave syrup
mint and lemon (optional)

Bring 6 cups of water to a boil. Add the Navajo tea and steep for 5–10 minutes. The tea will turn from a light golden color to a pretty amber and will depeen with flavor the longer it is steeped. Be careful not to steep to the point of bitterness. Stir in honey or agave syrup while still hot. Serve hot or let the tea cool, pour over ice, and garnish with mint or lemon, or both.

Edible Flowers

Hot, Bitter, and Wilted:
Flowers Protest

In 2016, as Donald Trump started campaigning for president, I began inviting bodega flower workers in New York City to make arrangements for him as a way to express their view on his immigration policies. I bought the arrangements made by the workers and interviewed them about their flower selections. Miguel, a native of Puebla, Mexico, who crossed the border in sixteen days nine years ago, didn't want to send anything fresh to Trump. He asked me if he could add flowers that were wilting, adding *"Que se pudra!"* ("That he rots!") He picked marigolds (a flower commonly used for the Day of the Dead), daisies, carnations, and hot pepper sticks (so that Trump would know the arrangement was from a Mexican).

His gesture of including edible flowers in their process of decay as well as peppers that characterize his traditional cuisine gets to the poetics and power of flowers. This natural symbol that activates our senses and helps us express our anger, joy, grief, hate, and love has been used as a tool of resistance for centuries, from indigenous folks using tinctures made from flowers such as chamomile to treat anxiety or inflammation, to wildflower seed bombs as a way of reclaiming public space in colonized land, to the movements against war and auto-cratic military power, including the flower power protests against the Vietnam War in the United States, the Carnation Revolution in Por-tugal, and the Rose Revolution in Georgia. Most recently, in April 13, 2021, women in Myanmar, who have led the protests against the military coup, marked Thingyan, the Burmese New Year, by marching with pots of padauk flowers—blooms that are typically used in the celebration of the holiday—in honor of those who were killed during the fight for a democratic government.

As an artist, I was interested not only in flowers as symbols of resistance, but also in expressing the differences that coexist in a flower arrangement. Similar to a recipe where a particular flower could be used as a garnish or as a coloring element in harmony with other ingre-dients, an arrangement becomes a source of communal representation. Eva, also a native of Puebla, crossed "El Cerro" twenty years ago and has never gone back. Her daughter, named Anahi after the flower, is a sixteen-year-old born in the United States to an undocumented parent. On Sundays, Anahi sells flowers with her mother. While making the arrangement, Eva mentioned how the rich couldn't understand the poor: *"El está en su torre y no tiene que mirar para abajo!"* ("He is in his tower, and he doesn't need to look down!") Eva's comment leaves me wonder-ing how Trump would react to these flower arrangements.

How would he taste the wilted daisies, carnations, and hot peppers in Miguel's arrangements if he ate them? Would the heat of the peppers combined with the bitterness of the daisies be enough vengeance for the distress of his years in office? I'll never know. But in the meantime, flowers will continue to help us express ourselves.

Urtica dioica

Nettle

Origin Eurasia, North Africa
Type Forb
Blooms Summer

Brushing up against a nettle is startling, as the tiny hairs on the plant inject a histamine into skin, stinging you, as its colloquial name, stinging nettle, implies. Its genus name, *Urtica*, also means "burn," a fair warning. Despite its prickly nature, the nettle plant has figured into many parts of daily life, as food, medicine, and clothing. There is an abundance of evidence of the nettle in early European history, dating from as far back as the late Bronze Age (around the thirteenth century BCE). One notable anecdote involves Julius Caesar's soldiers purposefully stinging themselves with the plant to stay alert. The nettle plant was also used historically to produce a textile similar to flax. The plant would be dried and woven into a green cloth that was useful as camouflage, but it was also bleached and dyed like cotton. Nettle fabric was common in sixteenth- and seventeenth-century Scottish households, and was also produced in twentieth-century Germany, especially during wartime periods in which cotton was in short supply.

The nettle, a subspecies of which is also native to North America, has played an important role in ceremonial practices for several Native American tribes: some Nevada tribes burned nettles in sweat lodges, and the Kawaiisu people would walk barefoot over nettles to cleanse themselves before entering the dreamworld.

The culinary uses of nettle are many. The French have used nettle in cheese-making, as a nettle decoction can curdle milk in a way similar to rennet. Steeping nettle in water, like a tea, produces a lively spring tonic that can be added to cordials and beer. Both the leaves and flowers—which are tiny and green—can be eaten with rice, cheese, fish, and poultry, and can be prepared simply by blanching. The leaves have even more vitamin C and iron than spinach.

Nigella damascena

Nigella

Origin Europe, North Africa
Type Forb
Blooms Spring

Nigella flowers have a fairy-tale-like quality to them; they seem almost to be make-believe. The flowers have spiky, pale blue or violet petals that blossom from a striped seedpod and are engulfed by thin, feathery greenery. The flower is also known as love-in-a-mist, which perfectly evokes the hazy universe created by a tangle of nigella. The plant is native to southern Europe and North Africa, and its specific epithet, *damascena* means "of Damascus." The seedpods hold a black seed that is often confused with black cumin or what are commonly called nigella seeds (which in fact come from *Nigella sativa*). The seeds of the *Nigella damascena* have a slight nutmeg flavor and can be ground and eaten while raw, or cooked. The flowers are also edible, but are best used ornamentally.

Images – pp. 184, 185

Abelmoschus esculentus

Okra Flower

Origin Africa
Type Forb
Blooms Summer

Okra blooms in the low heat of morning and lasts only one day. The okra flower is a creamy, pale yellow funnel with a dark reddish-brown center; it looks like an unfussy hibiscus with its color drained. (In fact, okra and hibiscus are members of the same family, Malvaceae.)

The okra plant is thought to have originated in Africa as early as the twelfth century BCE. For centuries it has been an important ingredient in African cuisines. In the United States, it is largely associated with the South, where it occupies a prominent place in the African culinary diaspora. It is believed that okra was introduced to the Americas via the transatlantic slave trade. Food activist Leah Penniman, the author of *Farming While Black*, tells the story of her ancestral grandmother braiding the seeds of millet, okra, black rice, and sorghum into

Edible Flowers

(Okra, cont.)

her hair before being forced onto a slave ship and stolen from her home in West Africa. As Penniman told the *Harvard Gazette*, "[She knew] there would be some seed we all needed to inherit. That's what our grandmothers did for us."

The name *okra* is thought to derive from the Nigerian Igbo word ọ́kụ̀rụ̀ and was first recorded in the colony of Virginia in 1679. Though the flowers are delicate, okra is a hardy vegetable that grows quickly and easily in the Southern soil and sustained enslaved communities for generations. Michael W. Twitty, author of *The Cooking Gene: A Journey through African-American Culinary History in the Old South*, writes, "In mainland North America, okra was one of the ultimate symbols of the establishment of the enslaved community as a culinary outpost of West Africa." Okra flower petals can accent dishes that incorporate okra, such as gumbo or curry, or be sautéed lightly. See Claire Ratinon's essay on okra flowers on page 141.

Images — pp. 140, 186

Dendrobium spp.

Orchid

Origin Asia, Australia
Type Forb
Blooms Spring

Orchids, which are so different from other flowers, can seem unnatural, as if developed by a mad scientist. Not all orchids are edible, particularly not the spiderlike hybrids, but all orchids within the genus *Dendrobium* can be eaten. The more pedestrian variety can be found packaged in grocery stores or sold in bulk for tropical cocktails. The bright magenta and white blossoms commercially known as karma orchids are the most common. Orchid flowers are dense and crisp like endive or watercress. They appear widely in Asian cuisine, often battered and fried, and in Hawaii they are added to salads and coated with sugar for dessert. In Turkey, ice cream known as *dondurma* gets its elasticity from salep powder, which is derived from the tubers of another genus of orchid, *Orchis*.

Edible Flowers

Viola × *wittrockiana*

Pansy

Origin Eurasia
Type Forb
Blooms Spring

The pansy is one of the most common edible flowers, included by garden writer, gourmet horticulturist, and doyenne of edible flowers Cathy Wilkinson Barash in her "big ten." The winsome flower is often seen on cakes and in salads and is typically included in packaged edible flowers sold in grocery stores. The face often identified in the flower is created by its five overlapping petals, which have dark smudges or whiskers at the center, giving the bloom the appearance of having eyes and a beard and the impression of being deep in thought. The flower's common name comes from the French word *pensée*, meaning "thought," and in the Victorian language of flowers, pansies were used to expresses the sentiment "thinking of you." The flower is referred to, though somewhat obliquely, in Shakespeare's *A Midsummer Night's Dream*, when Puck is sent to gather "a little western flower" that maidens call "love-in-idleness."

Viola × *wittrockiana*, the common, silver dollar–sized blossoms, were first illustrated and described to a British audience in 1831 in the pages of *English Botany*. The flower comes in a wide variety of colors, often bold red, purple, yellow, and black, and with variegated and multicolored petals in one flower. The whole flower is edible and has a wintergreen flavor; the petals alone have a slightly milder, grassy taste. It can be incorporated into cooking in many ways: baked onto shortbread cookies, added to salads or fish dishes, used to decorate canapés, and dipped in chocolate.

Images — pp. 169, 188

Pansy

When I was young, my mother would take me to stay at Rabbit Run, the family home of her childhood best friend, Cindy Lee. We would drive hours to get there, up from Miami's flat concrete heat through Central Florida, past the Big Cypress Seminole Reservation, swamp houses on stilts that gave way to strip malls set between sunny fields where saw grass stuttered in the breeze. I thought I saw wildcats on these drives, Florida's native golden panthers, rarely observed but in mascot logos. No one could tell me I didn't.

Rabbit Run felt like the estates in the historical fantasy my grandma bought from the Kmart book aisle—refined acreage best described as a gentleman's farm with stables, pastures, and gardens for the pleasure of its owners. Like the thrill of those cheap dramas, it set the scene for my dominant childhood sense memories: the prick of hay on my skin as I fell off the donkey Homer, his mate, Hannah, gazing at me indifferently from the corner of the pen; cicadas wailing all night; the scent of Spanish moss tangles, dripping from the trees after a rainstorm; the tang of pansy petals in butter lettuce salads served at dinner on the veranda.

The pansies were what really got me. I was shaken by the revelation that we could eat the flowers, not the bitter broccoli and artichokes packing the Publix produce shelves, but the vibrant pink perennials charming the window box. I remember pretending to the guests at the table that I knew pansies were edible, of course. I was eight or nine and terrified of being wrong. Of not having the answer. At the time, I thought of meaning as absolute. Finite. That truth was fully formed and discoverable, like four-leaf clovers in the grass. But after the pansies, I knew I would never be right.

Last night, I dreamt I was at Rabbit Run again, lying in the pasture weeds, waiting for a snake to slither up and bite. You know that feeling, like watching the girl descend dark basement stairs in a slasher film. The giddy vibration of apprehension, an intoxicating desire for catharsis. I told my therapist in his Coconut Creek office, faux-bois walls lined with poetry and Japanese ink drawings, arias blasting as he sat, eyes closed, in golf shorts. "Expectation is the killer of joy," he advised.

But isn't it the only thing that keeps us going? Expectation, not joy. The elemental understanding that in this world, we will be led by our senses, and that experience will shape us, has shaped us. That the gifts of the body may be better than those of the mind, as John Donne surmised. Certainty is only a performance of ignorance. The pansies teach us that.

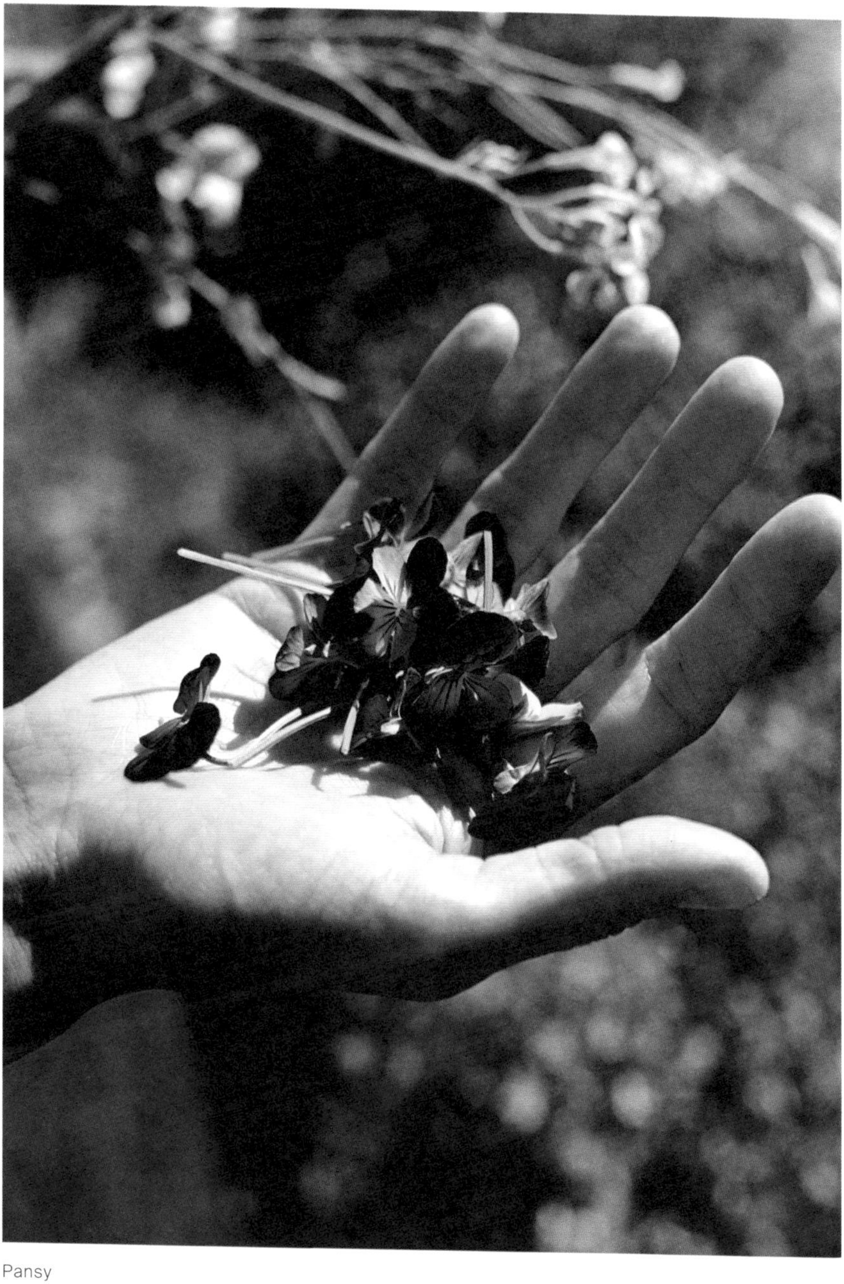

Pansy

Poppy

Edible Flowers

Passiflora spp.

Passionflower

Origin South America
Type Flowering vine
Blooms Summer

Passionflower is a dramatic and supernatural-looking flower that grows on tropical vines alongside the passion fruit. The name was given to the plant by fifteenth-century Jesuit missionaries in South America who assigned meaning to the parts of the flower that, for them, symbolized the Passion of Christ. The curly tendrils represented the whips used in the flagellation of Christ, the stigmas were the nails, the corona portrayed the crown of thorns, and the ten petals and sepals stood in for the apostles—excluding Judas, the betrayer, and Peter, the denier. The mystical blossoms bloom for only one day, and the flower is known to be dried and used for tea. However, it is thought to have mild sedative and psychotropic effects and should not be consumed in large quantities.

Paeonia spp.

Peony

Origin Eurasia, North America
Type Forb
Blooms Spring, summer

During its peak bloom and as it wilts, the peony is breathtaking in its lushness. Peony is one of the longest cultivated flowers in Asia. Known as "king of the flowers" in China, a peony plant can live to be over a hundred years old. Though the flower is today commonly considered ornamental, it is recorded in ancient texts as a foodstuff. Confucius is said to have exclusively eaten foods with peony. The petals, which have a sweet and slightly fruity flavor, are typically blanched or employed as a lavish garnish.

Image – p. 183

Edible Flowers

Phlox

Origin North America
Type Forb
Blooms Spring, summer

It should be noted that it is the tall perennial phlox, not the low-growing creeping phlox, that is edible. Native to the eastern United States, perennial phlox, also known as garden phlox, can grow up to four feet tall and bears fragrant tubular flowers that can be pink, purple, or white and are beloved by hummingbirds and butterflies. The flowers are mildly sweet and spicy.

Image – p. 191

Papaver spp.

Poppy

Origin Africa, Eurasia
Type Forb
Blooms Summer

The Sumerians, the earliest known civilization in Mesopotamia, referred to the poppy as the "joy plant." The poppy has always been a crowd-pleaser. And a particular joy can be found in the form of small black poppy seeds flavoring bagels (or simmered with honey, milk, sugar, and lemon juice to make filling for *hamantaschen* cookies and Eastern European sweet breads) or by watching the tousled blooms sway on comically thin stems. But the same flower that gives us the delicious seeds and stunning sights also contains toxic compounds that when ingested induce a feeling of euphoria—an effect that has been the main impetus for the flower's cultivation since the fourth millennium BCE. The opium poppy, *Papaver somniferum*, is thus the producer of the world's oldest drug, and compounds extracted from the plant are still used to create pain killers and illegal narcotics such as heroin. In modern cultural history, opium is often associated with the nineteenth-century literary world of the Romantics; the poets John Keats and Samuel Taylor Coleridge are said to have been addicted to

(Poppy, cont.)

opium, and the 1821 autobiographical book *Confessions of an English Opium-Eater* by Thomas De Quincey recounts the author's own struggles with the narcotic.

The field poppy, *Papaver rhoeas*, is less fraught, but should still be approached with caution. Most poppy species are quite toxic when ingested, and considering the harmful properties of parts of even the edible species of the flower, sorting the safe from the toxic requires extreme vigilance. Leave the work to the professionals and source your poppy seeds from the supermarket. The poppy flower is a joy to look at, nonetheless.

Images — pp. 170, 187, 189

Opuntia spp.

Prickly Pear

Origin North America
Type Forb
Blooms Summer

Native to the United States, prickly pear is the classic cactus of North America. Every part of it is edible, including its broad, flat pads, which are covered in long, fine thorns; the fleshy red fruit known as tuna; and the large yellow blossoms. The juicy tuna fruit, which can be eaten raw or cooked into jellies and jams, was among the few naturally sweet foods available to early Native Americans, such as the Ancestral Puebloans. In Mexico, prickly pear is known as nopal, and it is eaten in tacos and salads, or batter-fried like french fries. Grilled nopales are also essential to *parrillada*, mixed barbecue. Perhaps the greatest tributes to this cactus are that a village in central Mexico celebrates an annual festival, *la Feria del Nopal*, in its honor, and that Texas adopted the prickly pear as its state plant.

Primula vulgaris

Primrose

Origin Western Europe, United Kingdom
Type Forb
Blooms Summer

As many English botanists can attest, the primrose is ubiquitous in the United Kingdom, carpeting woodlands, pastures, and hedgerows. Over the years, this rosette-forming perennial had grown scarce, until countries such as Northern Ireland instituted protections that forbade the sale and removal of the species. *Primula vulgaris*, meaning "little earliest one," is an apt name for this perennial, which is known to burst forth in March and April after the dreary winter draws to a close. *Vulgaris*, meaning "common," is a nod to the plant's ability to thrive in a variety of habitats, from grasslands to forests. The primrose's fragrant flowers—usually a pale yellow color—are supported by short, single stems and bloom in clusters.

The primrose is often incorporated into both savory dishes and desserts. Its leaves and flowers can be served raw or cooked, adding a dash of flavor to any salad. With hints of sweetness, the flower has been made into teas, syrups, and even wine.

The flower holds a unique place in British history. In the United Kingdom, April 19 is Primrose Day, which commemorates the anniversary of former Prime Minister Benjamin Disraeli's death. It is said that Queen Victoria knew that the primrose was Disraeli's favorite flower and would send bunches of them to his residence. Upon hearing of the prime minister's death, the queen reportedly sent a wreath composed of primrose to be laid atop his coffin. It is now an annual tradition for the flower to be placed in front of Disraeli's sculpture outside Westminster Abbey on the anniversary.

Violets

Violets have always grown in my mother's garden. Their appearance preceded the arrival of spring—they were the modest harbingers of warmer weather to come. While the violets were flowering, I would tarry on my way in from school to collect a handful for my mother, visiting whichever plants I'd neglected the previous day. (She would tell me, in a reassuring tone, "They *like* to be picked!") Collecting a bouquet of violets became a ritual: new stems would refresh the tiny copper lusterware vase on the kitchen windowsill each day. As my mother arranged these, supplementing the previous day's harvest, she would deftly pluck out any faded or withered specimens as she went along. I loved rifling through the leafy underbrush of the garden, searching for the minuscule flowers that cowered beneath their lobed, heart-shaped leaves. I would be left alone in the yard, absorbed in my unhurried labor, the front door left ajar, an invitation to enter at my leisure. I delighted in offering this ephemeral arrangement to my mother—hemmed in a ring of dark green leaves after the manner of the Parisian flower vendors I'd heard about in stories—and she *always* delighted in receiving it. They are, as a result, a flower I will forever associate with her.

The violet is known throughout history to eulogize and commemorate, but also to decorate, perfume, salve, heal, and seduce. In ancient Greek mythology, violets were double edged: alluding to death and dying—mantling a funeral pyre in a miasma of fragrant purple—but also suggesting chastity, modesty, virginity. Artemis, it is said, transformed one of her nymph companions into a violet to protect the girl from her brother's amorous advances. Zeus made his lover Io's tears into scented violets to ease her melancholy at having been transformed by the god into a cow to protect her from his wife Hera's wrath. The purple flowers were plaited into crowns for maiden dances and festivals, collected in baskets to scent the home, sprinkled into steaming baths. When Sappho described a girl gathering or braiding violets, or delicately heaping violets in the gentle valley of her lap, she would generally have been alluding to the girl's purity or to her youth. But in another passage, we are given the memory of a girl whose innocence Sappho may *already* have taken, whose companionship Sappho has enjoyed, but lost. The violet, or the memory of it, becomes a taunt, then: the aroma of a vanished, bygone love.

When, in my twenties, I visited Keats's grave in the Protestant Cemetery on the outskirts of Rome, I found a carpet of violets at the foot of his headstone, a spangling of purple beneath the impossible-to-forget epitaph, *Here lies One Whose Name was writ in Water.* I remember stooping to pick a handful—a muscle memory, perhaps, from the days of gathering them for my mother—and pressed them between the pages of whatever book I was reading. I sent one, dried and flattened, glued carefully to a sheet of paper, along with a letter to a friend in Dublin, a boy I loved in a never-to-be-consummated kind of way.

In that moment, the violet expressed pure longing. I remember typing out, on my typewriter, the litany of names I'd learned for all the many related flowers that fall into Violaceae, the family that holds both the violet and the pansy: *heart's ease, bird's eye, bullweed, pink-eyed John, pink-of-my-Joan, wild pansy, love-lies-bleeding, love-in-idleness, love idol, cuddle me, call-me-to-you, meet-me-in-the-entry, three-faces-under-a-hood, Jack-jump-up-and-kiss-me, kiss-me-at-the-garden-gate...* But then, even when it came to the violet itself, further identifying questions were necessary. Were you referring to the dog violet (the kind that ribbons the cliffs of southern Ireland near our friends' home in Ballymaloe) or to the marsh violet, or perhaps to the hairy violet? The last are unscented, though nearly identical to the *Viola odorata*, the sweet violet. This was the variety my mother planted, the kind that, if pinned to a lapel, made a perfect, if fleeting, nosegay. If you find a profusion of this sweetly scented variety and are feeling industrious, candy the flowers.

Violet ice cubes

Portulaca oleracea

Purslane

Origin North Africa
Type Forb
Blooms Summer

In *Walden*, Henry David Thoreau recounts "a satisfactory dinner"
he made "simply off of a dish of purslane." This hardy plant, which
is rumored to have been one of Mahatma Gandhi's favorite foods, is
often considered, or dismissed, as a weed in North America. While it is
easy enough to find purslane's tear-shaped leaves cropping up through
sidewalk cracks, this annual succulent has many culinary applications
for a range of dishes, from soups and stews to salads and dips. Several
parts of the purslane plant are edible, including the leaves, stems, and
flowers. Known for its salty taste, purslane is best used when the leaves
are young; otherwise it takes on a bitter flavor with age.

Purslane is believed to be native to North Africa and has been harvested as a food source in countries around the world for thousands of
years. It is rich in vitamins A and C and boasts a high level of omega-3
fatty acids. This international plant goes by many names: *pourpier* in
French and *verdolaga* in Spanish. Purslane is a standard ingredient in
recipes like Lebanese *fattoush* salad, South Sudanese red lentil stew,
and Mexican pork neck with *verdolaga*.

Purslane's disc-like flowers typically open in bright sunlight and
close on overcast or rainy days. The rugged plant grows in dry soil and
can manage in severe drought.

Daucus carota

Queen Anne's Lace

Origin Europe
Type Forb
Blooms Summer

Queen Anne's lace spreads like a veil across fields in the heat of summer; its filigreed white flowers can also be seen standing waist high on roadsides in Europe and the United States. One of the most resilient and enduring flowers, Queen Anne's lace is the wild ancestor of the domesticated carrot, hence it's frequently referred to by its common name, the wild carrot. (Its taproot smells just like a garden carrot, too.)

While it's true that Queen Anne's lace is edible, it is often mistaken for elderflower or for its poisonous twin hemlock; thus the flower should be sourced from a knowledgeable forager or grower. The single tiny red or purple floret at the center of the white, flat-topped umbel is a marked characteristic of Queen Anne's lace. This wildflower is thought to be named after Queen Anne of Great Britain, who, as legend goes, pricked her finger as she was tatting lace, leaving on her handiwork a drop of blood.

Queen Anne's lace can infuse a woody-sweet flavor into stews, cakes, and even cocktails. Its leaves, roots, flowers, and seeds are edible and best used during the plant's first year. Cooks can try their hand at deep-frying the delicate flower clusters or incorporate them as an unexpected garnish or spice in desserts such as crème brûlée and carrot cake.

Image – p. 190

Cydonia oblonga

Quince

Origin Western Asia
Type Flowering shrub
Blooms Spring

Quince is a close cousin of the apple in the family Rosaceae, and the blossoms of the two plants can be similar. The quince tree blooms in spring before it begins to bear fruit and the petals of the quince flower are edible. But, like the fruit, which is typically astringent, they tend to be very tart. It is best to boil the petals and reduce the flower's essence in a vinegar, though they can be eaten raw in a salad.

As the fruit remains quite hard when grown in cooler climates, quince has fallen out of popularity in North America and Britain over the years and is today mostly grown ornamentally. But in the Mediterranean and tropical regions, where the fruits can ripen and become soft, quince fruit can be eaten from the tree. The fruit is also used to make jam and jellies (quince is high in pectin), including *dulce de membrillo*, or just *membrillo*, a firm quince jelly that is traditionally served with Manchego cheese in Spain, and is also popular in South America. In Chile, a dessert, *murta con membrillo*, is made by preserving Chilean guava—*murta*—with quince. Leaves of *Cydonia oblonga* are sometimes used like grape leaves to make Greek dolmas.

Image – p. 181

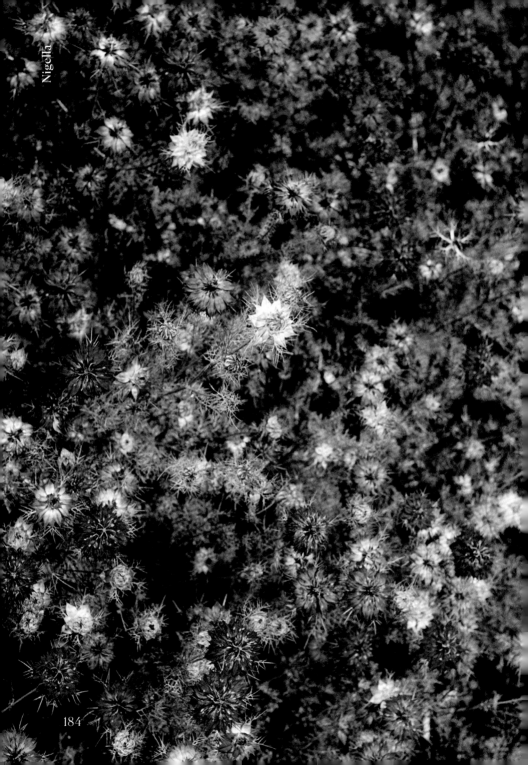

Nigella

Rose

Rosa spp.

Rose

Origin Eurasia, North America
Type Flowering shrub
Blooms Summer

Gertrude Stein said, "A rose is a rose is a rose." Perhaps she meant a rose is a macaron flavor, a rose is sold on the side of the road in giant bunches in February, a rose is the smell of antique stores, a rose is what we wished our skin felt like, a rose can cut you, a rose can change your day. But, even reduced to the plainest language, or the most quotidian, a rose eludes definition.

A rose will always surprise you. Someone has certainly said this before. Millions of words, feelings, and ideas have been given, and taken, from the rose, which is mostly due to its age, also in the millions. The rose is possibly one of the oldest flowers in the world, as indicated by a fossil of a bloom found in Colorado that dates back fifty-five million years. But age can't speak to alchemy, and the rose will never not enchant.

A deep crimson color is most associated with modern hybrid tea or grandiflora roses, though the flowering shrub can appear in a range of colors and sizes, some with deeper layers of velvety petals. All parts of the rose are edible, but it is best to choose older and heirloom varieties when eating the flowers. The growing and cultivating conditions of contemporary hybrids are less reliable. Commonly associated with love, the rose is often sexualized as an aphrodisiac. But it has long been used culinarily, as evidence of a rose wine from Persia dates back almost two thousand years. The rose spread to Europe during the Crusades and was used in the tenth century to prepare meat and poultry. Using rose water and rosebuds in cooking became increasingly popular during the Renaissance, which is explored in food historian Dave Dewitt's book *Da Vinci's Kitchen: A Secret History of Italian Cuisine.*

The flavor of the rose is fruity and sweet, reminiscent of strawberries or green apples, with a bit of warm spice. Generally, the darker the petal, the more pronounced the flavor. The essence of the flower remains a common ingredient in Middle Eastern and Indian dishes. It is the main flavoring of Turkish delight and the North African spice mix *ras el hanout* often includes dried rose petals.

(cont.)

Edible Flowers

(Rose, cont.)

Miniature roses can be candied and preserved to adorn cookies and cakes. Rose petals can also be used as one pleases—sprinkled across berries or simply dissolved on the tongue. Read Anna Morton's meditation on the rose on page 195.

Images — pp. 16, 192, 197

Rosmarinus spp.

Rosemary

Origin Mediterranean
Type Flowering shrub
Blooms Spring

The slim, spindle-like leaves of rosemary have a pungent, herbal fragrance unlike almost anything else. The hardy herb originates in the Mediterranean region and thrives wherever the climate is hot and humid. The name rosemary comes from the Latin words *ros*, "dew," and *marinus*, "sea." In Mediterranean cuisines, it is used both fresh and dried to flavor potatoes, eggs, and grilled or roasted meats, especially chicken. It is also distilled into an aromatic olive oil. Italian butchers often add complimentary sprigs of rosemary to their packages, and it is one of the five herbs typically found in the French *bouquet garni*, a bundle of fresh herbs used to flavor stocks and stews. Much like lavender, rosemary's sweet blueish-purple flowers can be made into a fragrant sugar or a floral butter. Rosemary is believed to enhance memory and cognition; in many cultures it symbolizes remembrance.

Rose

People underestimate the rose. We think of it as gentle, but it's one of the most potent of all the flowers, its oil one of the most powerful herbal medicines. The oil of rose contains more chemical constituents than any other essential oil and is used to treat a variety of ailments— infections, burns, hemorrhage, shingles, hormonal imbalance, anxiety, listlessness, libido.

Full of beauty and protective energy, the rose invokes the essence of Mother. Years ago, a friend was prescribed rose when trying to conceive. She was told to use rose in all its forms—to apply rose oil to her skin, bathe with the petals, drink a tea of the blossoms. She was pregnant within the year.

1. To Tend and Surrender

My first memory of roses is in my grandmother's rose garden. The garden was enclosed by a chest-high hedge at the far end of her swimming pool. She told me recently that we planted the roses together, though I have no memory of it. I do remember watching her tend them. She would deadhead the discolored ones, her own head and shoulders floating above the hedge line. She said the Japanese beetles liked the white roses more than the red ones. So the following year she grew only red. She said she learned quickly that one must protect roses from any number of things—whiteflies, aphids, black spot, mildew, hot weather, cold weather, and deer. She said it was worth it. She loved her roses.

2. To Encounter a Rose

Encounter a rose in the morning when its scent is most giving.

Ask a rose if it wants to be picked before you pick it. The rose will likely answer yes, as its nature is generous and its desire is to envelop you.

Never pick a rose in the heat of the day, only in early morning or at dusk. It is said a rose can suffer if picked when the sun is high.

If you decide to cultivate roses, choose from the heirloom varieties such as gallica, Damask, alba, centifolia, Cécile Brünner, or Noisette. They carry the most medicine and offer the purest fragrance.

The more I encounter roses the more I crave them.
Like an obsession. Like falling in love.
First observing from a distance. The color. The shape.
The velvet petals that curl and embrace.
Then noticing the scent that pulls me in.
A scent that instantly intoxicates, soothes, liberates, caresses.
I willingly enter the orbit of a rose and fall into her gravity.

I like to enjoy a rose simply by picking a petal and placing it on my tongue. The petal slowly melts and imparts its overflowing flavor.

I feel like a flower myself.

Rose

Crocus sativus

Saffron

Origin Crete
Type Forb
Blooms Summer

The flowering crocus flower known as saffron (not to be confused with its toxic relative, autumn crocus, of the genus *Colchicum*) contains just three bright red stigmas that are harvested by hand, each strand delicately plucked. With just a pound made from seventy-five thousand flowers, it's no wonder the laborious endeavor makes saffron the world's most expensive spice.

Wild saffron flowers are thought to have originated in Crete, and were reportedly used by ancient Greek and Roman civilizations. It was around that time that the flower was domesticated and saffron's ever-burgeoning uses found their way to Asia and Europe, serving alongside cinnamon and tea as a catalyst for the exchange of art, architecture, science, philosophy, and ideas. Always a lofty status symbol among the rich and powerful, Cleopatra is said to have bathed in a quarter-cup of saffron, and ancient Romans are said to have stuffed their pillowcase with it to prevent a hangover.

Saffron flowers grow from an underground corm, or bulb, and have thin, blade-like green leaves that can grow to sixty centimeters in length. The flowers range in color from light lavender to a deep royal purple. Some crocus bulbs will occasionally produce a pure white flower, which represents its original wild form. Saffron flowers have a sweet, honey fragrance, and the stigmas have a musky, hay-like, floral scent with an earthy note. When used as a dye or cooked in food, it produces a luminous golden coloring.

Today, most of the world's supply of saffron comes from Iran and has become an essential part of culinary culture worldwide. In Spain, no credible chef would endeavor to make a paella without the best saffron. For their part, Persians created their own classic staple, infusing ice cream with it, creating a pale yellow creamy cloud.

Salvia officinalis

Sage

Origin Mediterranean
Type Forb
Blooms Spring

In ancient Rome, China, and Egypt, and for centuries after, sage has been thought to have spiritual and medicinal healing properties. Both eating and burning dried sage has been used to ward off disease and improve mood. The herb's soft, furry leaves taste warm and peppery when cooked or dried, with flavors similar to eucalyptus and mint (p. 157). Like rosemary, sage originates in the Mediterranean region and is used interchangeably with the herb to flavor fatty meats such as pork. A popular culinary marriage is sage fried in browned butter, which lends a glossy-golden, nutty-earthy depth to pasta and chicken dishes. The British have embraced this Mediterranean herb as their own and use it on nearly everything, from vegetables to offal to scones. In the United States and Canada, sage can be found in the traditional Thanksgiving stuffing for turkey. Add sage's small lavender flowers to bring color to your holiday table.

Tragopogon porrifolius

Salsify

Origin Mediterranean
Type Forb
Blooms Spring

Salsify is a tall, spiky, prehistoric-looking wildflower, with a blossom that is generally considered ornamental for its straw-like texture, but is fully edible. Salsify's root is long, hardy, and pale white, like a parsnip. Its shoots are less dense than a parsnip or carrot, and can be cooked like an asparagus—steamed or gently roasted. The sprouted seeds are also used in salads or sandwiches.

Edible Flowers

Snapdragon

Few flowers inspire the imagination quite like the snapdragon, as children worldwide gently squeeze the sides of the flower to open and close the flower's "dragon's mouth." Its Latin species name, *Antirrhinum majus*—from the Greek words *anti*, meaning "like," and *rhis*, meaning "nose"—alludes to the flower's dragon-like snout, which snaps open and shut with a pinch of its head. A favorite of the bees, butterflies, and hummingbirds, the two-lipped perennial thrives in full sun and prefers well-drained soil.

Depending on its variety, the flower may be pink, purple, lavender, white, yellow, orange, or burgundy. The flower blooms along a long green stem and opens from the bottom to the top. The petals have a ruffled edge with a delicate, soft texture. The snapdragon's bitter taste might not rank it among the most flavorful of the edible flowers, but it makes for a splashy garnish atop a tart or a leafy salad with its rich color palette, ranging from pastels to bright, bicolor shades. Nota bene: A favorite Victorian parlor game played on Christmas Eve shares the same name ("Snap-dragon"), and involves seizing raisins from a bowl of burning brandy and then popping the flaming-hot fruit in your mouth.

Images – pp. 201, 220

Snapdragon

Edible Flowers

Squash blossom

Edible Flowers

Pisum sativum

Snap Pea

Origin Asia
Type Forb
Blooms Spring

Snap peas, also called sugar snap peas, are edible pea pods similar to snow peas (a related variety), but with a thicker, more watery pod that is crisp and juicy to the bite. There is a natural sweetness to the snap pea, hence the "sugar" in its other common name. Though the pod is mostly harvested and sold in bulk in the summer, the leaves, stem, curly tendrils, and blossom are also edible. The tender flowers, which have two white petals that curve inward almost like a conch shell, can add a subtle sweetness to salads.

Image – p. 221

Cucurbita pepo

Squash Blossom

Origin Mexico
Type Forb
Blooms Summer

The bright orange and yellow star-shaped squash blossoms bloom on the vine with zucchini and yellow squash in summer. The blossoms are paper-thin with some elasticity. On the vine they are open and when harvested, they close, making them the perfect vessel to stuff with fresh cheeses such as ricotta, then batter and fry. The earliest evidence of the domestication of the squash was found in a cave in Oaxaca, Mexico, that dates as far back as eight to ten thousand years ago. Squash was a food source for people native to the Americas for millennia. The word *squash* comes from the Narragansett word *askutasquash*, meaning "eat raw or uncooked." Each vine blossoms prolifically, producing dozens of flowers. The squash flower is a favorite seasonal food in cooler climates and remains an integral part of Mexican cooking. Fresh blossoms are used in quesadillas and omelets, and can be deep-fried, tossed across pizzas, or added to stews and salads.

Images – pp. 202, 219

Edible Flowers

Fragaria spp.

Strawberry Blossom

Origin Pan-global
Type Forb
Blooms Spring

Fragaria is a genus in the rose family, and there is a resemblance between strawberry flowers and roses: both generally have five round, radially symmetrical petals. All species of strawberry produce small white or yellow flowers early in their growth cycle. After the strawberry flower is pollinated, its bright yellow center becomes the fruit—as the petals fall away, the center fades to green and swells, slowly becoming red and taking shape as the beloved scarlet, heart-shaped fruit. The whole strawberry plant is edible, though the blossoms and leaves pale in flavor compared to the sweet, juicy fruit. You can harvest a few flowers and toss them on a sundae, but keep in mind that plucking a flower prevents a strawberry.

Image – p. 205

Strawberry

Edible Flowers

Sunflower

Edible Flowers

Helianthus annuus

Sunflower

Origin North America
Type Forb
Blooms Summer

True to its name, the sunflower is a faithful follower of the sun and particularly notable for its large, disc-shaped head and bright orange-yellow petals. This heliotropic plant begins its day facing east toward the rising sun and then follows the light, turning west as the sun sets. (It then reorients back to the east during the night.) Once the flower matures, however, it settles into a permanent position gazing east. Its genus name derives from the Greek words *helios*, meaning "sun," and *anthos*, meaning "flower." In Mexico, the Aztecs referred to the sunflower by several Nahuatl names—including *chimalacatl*, "shield reed," and *chimalxochitl*, "shield flower"—because of its physical likeness to the shields they used in battle. As a result, sunflower heads were often used as a sacred symbol to represent warfare. The earliest depiction of a sunflower, which can be found at the National Museum of Anthropology in Mexico City, is a pre-Hispanic stone sculpture of a sunflower head symbolizing the goddess Xochiquetzal. For centuries, the sunflower has also played muse to artists like Claude Monet and Vincent van Gogh.

Sunflower seeds are commonly consumed as a snack, as in trail mix, or in bread; its oil is frequently used for sautéing and baking. Chef Sean Sherman incorporates the seeds in his signature sunflower cookie recipe featured in his book *The Sioux Chef's Indigenous Kitchen*; Daniel Humm of famed restaurant Eleven Madison Park has been known to offer braised sunflower on his menu; and Chef Jaime Young has topped his black sea bass crudo with teddy bear sunflower petals at the eatery Sunday in Brooklyn.

Sunflowers are thought to have been domesticated four thousand years ago by Native Americans in eastern North America and brought to Europe by the Spaniards in the sixteenth century.

Images – pp. 206, 218

Artemisia dracunculus

Tarragon

Origin Eurasia
Type Forb
Blooms Summer

In the thirteenth century, the Spanish-Arabian botanist Ibr Baithar became one of the first people to draw attention to the distinctive flavor of tarragon, a native of Europe and Asia, though specifically presumed to be from Siberia. At times called wild or Russian tarragon, it is also known as the dragon herb or *herbe au dragon* in French. Much of the association with dragons comes from the serpentine shape of the herb's roots. But it's the French variety (var. *sativa*) that is best known for its culinary qualities.

The herb is an ardent favorite among chefs. The late James Beard, whose name is associated with one of culinary world's most prestigious awards, once said, "I believe that if ever I had to practice cannibalism, I might manage if there were enough tarragon around."

The leafy green herb and its orange flowers have a warm and subtle taste that is particularly well suited to use with fish and chicken and as part of vinaigrettes and sauces. Tarragon is one of the main ingredients in *chakapuli*, a Georgian national dish. And in Iran, tarragon is used as a side dish in *sabzi khordan* ("fresh herbs") or in stews and in Persian-style pickles, particularly *khiar shoor*. In Slovenia, tarragon is used in a variation of the traditional nut roll sweet cake, called *potica*. In Hungary a popular chicken soup known as *tárkonyos csirkeragu leves* defines itself by tarragon.

Image – p. 223

Thymus spp.

Thyme

Origin Mediterannean
Type Forb
Blooms Summer

The pronounced herbal flavor and aroma of thyme are significant to cuisines spread across the world, including British, Mediterranean, African, Latin American, and Caribbean. Thyme is similar to rosemary in its Mediterranean origins, and resembles oregano in taste, but it is gentler and blends more easily with a variety of flavors. Thyme is an essential part of the French *bouquet garni* and the herbal liqueur Bénédictine, which is flavored with a secret blend of twenty-seven flowers, herbs, and spices. In the Middle East and northern Africa, thyme is an important ingredient in za'atar, a spice mix that also contains toasted sesame seeds and sumac, and in Sicily, it is the basis for thyme honey, a tribute to how much bees love the plant's white or purple tubular flowers. It flavors the classic British dish jugged hare, a stew of hare cooked in a clay jug or casserole. The delicate herb also had some unconventional uses: it was used by ancient Egyptians in the process of embalming mummies.

Image – p. 246

Tulipa spp.

Tulip

Origin Eurasia
Type Forb
Blooms Spring

Though its life span in a vase may seem short, the tulip is actually rather hardy and responsive. After a brief slump, it can pick itself back up with fresh water or a shift in location. This showy flower has a lot of stories to tell. It originated in Persia, most likely Turkey, where it has long been a symbol of undying love. In Iran, the tulip is also given as the strongest sign of adoration. The bulbs have long been valued, spurring the seventeenth-century "tulip mania" in Holland, when European travelers were so enamored by the flower that prices soared to today's equivalent of thousands of dollars for a single bulb. Holland remains the primary exporter of tulips today, and its color-saturated fields are a wonder to behold from above.

All parts of the tulip are edible, including the bulbs, which were consumed as root vegetables amidst food shortages after World War II. Today, the petals are widely appreciated, with a bright lettuce-like flavor and a watery, cucumber texture. The size and shape, very scoop-like, make them perfect containers for dips and in salads, similar to an endive.

Images — pp. 211, 224

Tulip

Edible Flowers

Violet

Edible Flowers

Viola odorata

Violet

Origin Eurasia
Type Forb
Blooms Spring

Sappho wrote "all the violet tiaras, braided rosebuds, dill and crocus twined around your young neck." The ancient Greek poet penned the lines on papyrus from the island of Lesbos, a location deeply associated with love between women. Whether a crown of violets sent to a lover, or a Violet Quill—a name adopted by a group of gay writers in New York City in the 1980s—to many, sweet, wild violet represents desire of a fierce and saccharine caliber.

Wild violet, sometimes confused with its cousin the pansy (p. 166), has thin heart-shaped petals that are a vibrant purple-blue. They grow in early spring, covering the ground in shadier areas, reappearing faithfully each year. The flower has been cultivated for centuries and is native to Asia and Europe. It is also the symbol of Athens. *The Complete Book of Violets* by Nelson Coon links the plant to Hippocrates's journals from 446 BCE, which credit the flower's medicinal purposes, for example, to induce sleep and to calm the heart and mind. The Romans lavished themselves in violets, covering banquet tables and making wine from the blossoms, which they also drank the morning after to cure hangovers.

The scent of violets is strong yet fleeting. It has infused perfumes and candy, particularly *Violettes de Toulouse*, a tourist favorite of that city in the South of France. Violets grew immensely popular during the Victorian era when the scent and flower were almost inescapable—used in bridal nosegays, syrups, candies, soaps, and cosmetics. The French are still quite fond of the purple blossom, baking them into cakes and other sweets and using them to flavor ice creams, scones, and even marshmallows.

Images – pp. 2, 177, 212, 225

Nymphaea odorata

Water Lily

Origin North American
Type Forb
Blooms Spring, summer, fall

The water lily and lotus (p. 136) are very closely related. There are slight differences in the appearances and growth habits of the flowers: the water lily typically grows more quickly than the lotus and has larger, more fragrant flowers. Its petals are also slightly thicker than the lotus's, but, as with the lotus, its root is the part of the plant that is most commonly enjoyed.

Image – p. 152

Oxalis corniculata

Wood Sorrel

Origin Eurasia
Type Forb
Blooms Spring

Wood sorrel is a hardy and delicious weed, identifiable by its shamrock-shaped leaves (which should only be eaten in small quantities). Its genus name, *Oxalis*, from the Greek word *oxys*, meaning "sour" or "sharp," references the acidic notes of its flavor profile. In the *Handbook of Edible Weeds*, James A. Duke writes of the many ways that native peoples of North American used species of *Oxalis*, including for medicinal purposes. For example, the people of the Potawatomi tribe made a dessert of *Oxalis* cooked with sugar. Wood sorrel flowers can be added to pizzas, salads, and sauces. A few flowers can also be sprinkled on a creamy sorrel soup.

Images – pp. 5, 226

Yarrow, chamomile, broccoli, and fennel flowers found
in July at Union Square Greenmarket in New York.

Achillea millefolium

Yarrow

Origin Eurasia
Type Forb
Blooms Summer

In summer, the meadows alongside country roads are scattered with the lacy white, pink, and yellow flowers of yarrow, an ancient bitter herb. The origins of yarrow have been traced back tens of thousands of years: remnants of the plant were found in the Shanidar Cave of Iraq, where a Neanderthal was buried with flowers, including yarrow. The plant has since been naturalized in countries around the world and today is abundant in the eastern and central parts of the United States and Canada.

Its Latin name, *Achillea millefolium*, derives from Achilles, who is said to have kept yarrow with him to cure battle wounds. The Navajo people chewed the plant for toothaches and used it to treat earaches. In folklore, women in Ireland would place a bunch of the plant under their pillow the eve of May Day and recite "Good morrow, good yarrow, good morrow to thee / I hope by the yarrow my lover to see." In China, yarrow stalks represent the perfect universal balance of yin and yang.

Yarrow is a hearty plant that typically grows to two or three feet tall. Each stem has multiple flat flower heads comprising microclusters of fifteen to forty disk-shaped flowers surrounded by three to eight white-to-pink ray petals. Yarrow's fernlike foliage is soft and feathery when young but can become quite sharp and prickly with maturity. Both the leaves and flowers have a spicy herbal aroma that is reminiscent of crushed rosemary and oregano, starting off sweet and honeyed and finishing with a clean, bitter bite.

Yarrow's bitter quality is similar to that of hops (p. 127) and may be used for flavoring beer. When young, the leaves and blossoms can be eaten raw, but should be used sparingly due the bitter finish. The flower may be steeped as tea or used to infuse oil. The blossoms add a honey note to ice creams and gelati. Cooking can amplify its bitterness. When fresh, yarrow complements other soft, leafy herbs such as tarragon, chervil, parsley, and chive. When dried, the flavor becomes intense and earthy, making a better accompaniment to sage, thyme, and oregano.

Images – pp. 215, 217, 227

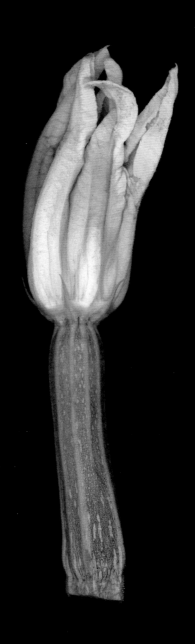

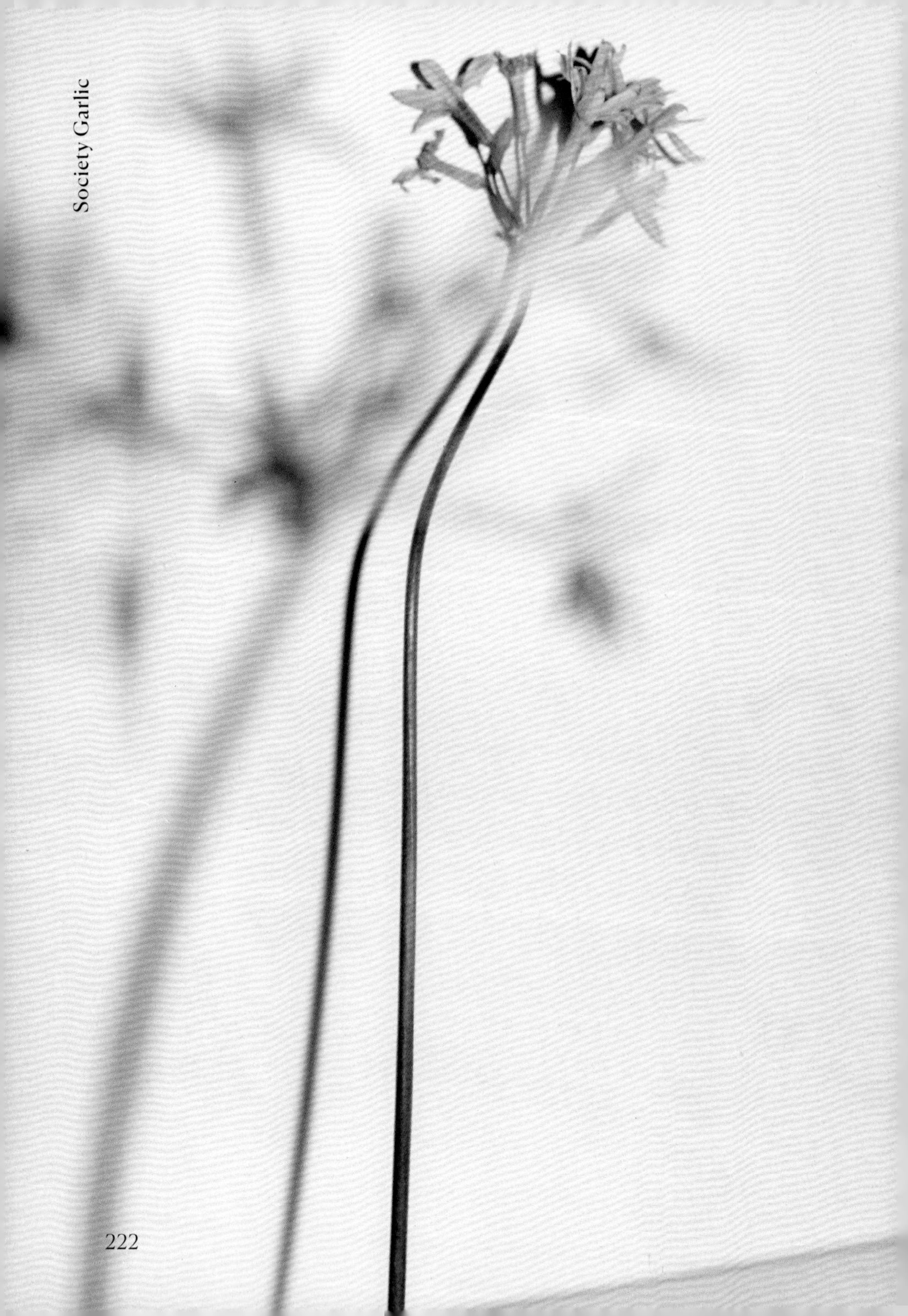

Zinnia

Yucca baccata

Yucca

Origin Mexico
Type Forb
Blooms Spring

The yucca is a prominent ingredient in Native American cooking, as well as Mexican, where its flower is called *flor de izote*. The large drought-resistant plant has tough leaves in the shape of swords and a large panicle of star-shaped ivory blossoms. The flower has a mildly sweet taste that is sometimes compared to green peas or asparagus, and also a bit of a crunch. Only the petals are used in cooking, as the rest of the plant is toxic. The flowers are in full bloom in the spring, and they can be used in salads raw, or lightly sautéed.

See Aurora Robles's recipe for Battered Flores de Izote on page 240.

Zinnia elegans

Zinnia

Origin Central America
Type Forb
Blooms Summer

Clementine Hunter, a self-taught painter who lived and worked at Melrose Plantation in Louisiana after Reconstruction, painted numerous still lifes of zinnias in everyday vases and pots. Arrangements of the colorful blossoms were one of her favorite subjects, which inspired the title of the 2013 opera *Zinnias: The Life of Clementine Hunter*, directed by Robert Wilson and written by Jacqueline Woodson.

Native to Central America, the zinnia bears flowers that are typically bright orange, yellow, or magenta and have several layers of oval-shaped petals, sometimes of alternating or ornamental patterns. The petals of the zinnia flower are edible but slightly bitter and best used as decoration on cakes or sweets or tossed into a salad for color.

Image – p. 228

Edible Flowers

Cooking with Flowers

Edible Flowers

Cultured Butter with Flowers
Chula Galvez

A very good way to preserve fresh edible flowers is with fat. Fat will not only retain the flowers' vibrant colors and shapes, but will also absorb the flowers' flavor. I love making cultured butter with flowers to eat with bread. It has the nutty flavor of butter, but with a slight tang. And with the flowers' taste and colors, it's perfect.

There are two ways to make cultured butter: you can use milk kefir grains or good-quality plain yogurt. If using milk kefir grains, add heavy cream to the grains in a clean glass jar and cover with a kitchen towel. Set the jar in the warmest place in your house, such as close to a heater or in the kitchen, for 30–48 hours. The longer you leave it, the tangier your butter will be.

Strain the milk, rescuing the kefir grains to use again, and let it cool in the fridge. You now have crème fraîche (and it's delicious to eat like this too).

If using plain yogurt, follow the same procedure as with kefir grains, but use 5 percent of the heavy cream's weight of yogurt (if you have 1 liter of heavy cream, you will use 50 grams of yogurt).

Once your crème fraîche is cold and ready, using an electric mixer, mix well on high until yellow curds begin to form in the buttermilk. Separate the buttermilk and discard it, or save it to use in a cake recipe.

Collect the yellow butter solids and place them in a large bowl with cold water and ice. Knead the butter in the ice water as long as possible. This will allow the rest of the buttermilk to dissolve in the water and result in a clean butter. Remove the butter from the water and, if you like, add some sea salt.

Spread plastic wrap on a work surface and place edible flowers face down. (If you use aromatic edible flowers, that flavor will pass to the butter.) Spread the butter on top of the edible flowers. Add more flowers to the top of the butter face up and cover with more plastic wrap.

Refrigerate the butter until hard. It will last up to 1 month in the fridge (and the flowers' flavor will get stronger with time) and up to 3 months in the freezer.

Enjoy.

Flower Vinegar

Hopping Clover Kombucha

Flower Vinegar
Christina Crawford

6 tbsp fresh or dried edible flowers
1 cup sugar
3 quarts boiled water
¼ tsp champagne yeast
vinegar mother or 1 cup raw vinegar

To a 1-gallon sterilized glass container with a wide rim, add the fresh or dried flowers in any combination you like. I used chamomile, hibiscus, and rose. Add the sugar and carefully add the boiling water. Steep overnight or for a few nights.

Add the yeast and stir to combine. Cover the container with a clean cloth and store it away from sunlight. Wait a few weeks until it ferments.

Add the raw vinegar or vinegar mother. Cover the container again, label it, and store out of sunlight, but at room temperature; if it gets too cold, it will go dormant. When the liquid tastes like vinegar, strain out the solids.

Bottle it and give it away.

Hopping Clover Kombucha
Tara Thomas

I'm no fermentation expert, but what I love about it is the process. The outcome is dependent on the intention you put into it.

While living in the forest in Norway for about two months, I consumed much of my surroundings through daily foraging trips and harvesting from the garden. Earlier that year, while I was in New York, I'd collaborated with my friend Christina Crawford, a fermentation queen who is the mind behind Tart Vinegar. We created a crimson clover vinegar from red clover growing in my community garden—the flavors were oh so sweet and full of nectar. At that moment I didn't yet know the power of flowers and especially what fermentation can unlock and preserve from them. Now, in a nearby field, wild clover grew in clusters of pink pom-poms. Clover was the perfect candidate from experience and nostalgia. I collected about half an ounce.

Up on the barn there was a tall hops vine that had been there as long as my partner could remember. I had noticed they were blossoming and every day I would observe them for signs that they had peaked. One day I noticed the perfume that wafted from them during a rainstorm as I walked by. It was time to harvest. I gathered about half an ounce.

My intentions with this kombucha were to draw on my experiences to create and experiment, and to use ingredients that were 100 percent local or wild. I also wanted to explore a higher sugar content to create a sweeter yet carbonic beverage. I learned from Christina that flowers have so much flavor in them, a few can go a long way—especially in fermentation.

½ oz each clover and hops flowers
2 cups beet or cane sugar
kombucha scoby
kombucha starter

Shake the clover and hops flowers to rid their petals of any dirt, then rinse them lightly without washing off too much of the flavors locked inside.

Fill a large pot with just over 2 liters of water (this will account for evaporation) and bring to a boil. Remove it from the heat and add the flowers.

Steep the flowers for 30 minutes, then remove them from the pot. Add 2 cups of beet sugar or cane sugar, then stir the liquid to dissolve. Allow the tea to cool to room temperature.

Place the kombucha scoby and a bit of kombucha starter into a clean 2-liter jar, then fill with the new tea! Cover with a cloth tightly secured with a rubber band or string. Label the jar with the date, contents, and name. Store in a cool, dark place. Feel free to taste once a week; for me, at twenty days it was superb! Floral, bright, and transcendent, with intense carbonation.

Two Flower Salads
Adrianna Glaviano

Herb and Flower Salad

Cilantro and parsley make up the base of this salad and other fresh, leafy herbs such as dill, mint, tarragon, basil, or chive may be added in smaller quantities as their stronger flavors can overpower it.

1 bunch of cilantro, roughly chopped
½ bunch flat-leaf parsley, roughly chopped
sprigs of other fresh and strongly flavored herbs, roughly chopped
juice of 1 lime
2 tbsp extra-virgin olive oil
pinch of cumin
pinch of chili flakes
sea salt
bit of feta, crumbled
smoked trout filet (optional)
handful of flowers to garnish

Combine the herbs. For a more delicate salad, remove the leaves from their stems.

To make the dressing, in a small bowl combine the lime juice, olive oil, cumin, and chili flakes and whisk until well combined. Add salt to taste.

After dressing the greens, I like to sprinkle a bit of feta over the salad to round out the flavors, and even some-times add a smoked trout filet that I shred with my hands. Finally, garnish the salad with the flowers of cilantro, mint, chive, or garlic, or other tender edible blooms.

Leafy Greens and Blossoms

This is a very simple salad that makes a big impression with the addition of flowers. This version is composed of quince, apple blossoms, and a mix of spring greens, but it can be made with any leafy greens and any edible flowers.

1 quince, cored and thinly sliced
spring greens or other leafy greens
handful of apple blossoms
vinegar
olive oil
salt and pepper
pinch of sumac powder

Mix the greens and quince, then add the apple blossoms and with your hands gently combine.

To make the dressing, in a small bowl whisk the vinegar and olive oil until well combined and season to taste with salt and pepper. Dress the salad and sprinkle a large pinch of sumac.

Cooking with Flowers

Edible Flowers

Candied Violets
Fanny Singer

My favorite thing to do with candied violets is to rim the edge of a lemon curd tart, giving it a candied violet crown. Candying flowers is one of those things that make an enormous, lasting impression on guests, though is quite easily undertaken.

Line a baking tray with waxed paper. In a medium bowl, whisk 1 large egg white just until frothy. Place 1 cup of superfine sugar in a small bowl. Using tweezers, take one violet at a time by the stem (be certain to use the edible common purple violet, which grows both cultivated and wild), dip it into the egg white, covering all surfaces, give it a tap, then carefully dip it into the sugar, being sure to coat the whole flower.

Place each flower on the prepared baking sheet and use a toothpick or a small knife to coax the flower back into its original shape. Fill in any uncoated patches with a tiny additional sprinkle of sugar. Trim the stems.

Allow the flowers to dehydrate in a warm, dry area for 24–36 hours. Once completely dry, store them in an airtight container and keep them for up to 2 months.

Rose Syrup
Laila Gohar

I like to have this at home to add to a little sparkling water or almond milk. Both rose and orange blossoms remind me of the desserts I grew up eating in Egypt. Many dairy-based Middle Eastern desserts have rose syrup, while pastries tend to be soaked in orange blossom syrup.

Simple syrup is really easy to prepare: it is equal parts sugar and water. To make the rose simple syrup, combine 1 cup of sugar and 1 cup of water in a small pan and bring to a boil over medium heat. Then add the juice of 1 lemon. Reduce the heat and add the petals of about a dozen roses. (When buying roses to be eaten, make sure to buy food-safe flowers that are not sprayed with pesticides). Let the syrup steep for 20 minutes, then strain and keep in a glass jar in the fridge.

Cooking with Flowers

Battered Flores de Izote
(*Flores de Izote Capeadas*)
Aurora Robles

The national flower of El Salvador, flor de izote, the flower produced by yucca plants in spring and summer, is most often associated with Central American gastronomy. The Nahuatl word *izotl* (from which *izote* is derived) suggests it should also be identified with regional Mexican gastronomy, and there are numerous ways it is prepared in both cuisines. In Los Angeles, where it is common to see yucca plants in the landscaping, a sharp eye will notice the flowers sold by the stalk on street corners in neighborhoods that have predominantly Mexican and Central American communities. Like many flowers produced by succulents, the flor de izote's beauty is riotous; a chandelier, or inverted waterfall of creamy, cup-shaped blossoms dangling from an upright stalk that emerges from a plant with sword-shaped leaves. Many recipes call for blanching or boiling the flowers, but coating them in batter preserves their vegetal bite, reminiscent of artichokes or asparagus.

Find a stalk with a large cluster of flowers, and snip the flowers from the base of their thin stems (these will help later when dipping the flowers in the batter). Wash and dry the flowers. Lightly open the petals—they will snap off if this is not done gingerly—and, with utmost care, gently remove the pistils. Set them aside.

In a bowl, combine one part unbleached cake flour, one part sparkling water, and a pinch of salt. Add a few ice cubes to keep the batter cold.

Heat a neutral oil of your choice (rapeseed, peanut, sunflower, etc.) in a stainless steel pan. Dribble a small amount of the batter into the hot oil to check the heat. If the batter bubbles up immediately, the oil is at the right temperature. Dip the flowers into the batter, holding them by the stem, and tap them on the edge of the bowl to remove excess batter. Gently add them to the hot oil (the oil should not be too hot, and the flowers should not be wet, or the oil will splash). Using chopsticks, flip them after about 10 seconds. Remove the flowers before they start to brown; fried evenly, they should be light yellow in color, with perhaps some browned edges. Place them on a tray lined with newspaper and paper towels to absorb the oil. Dust with dried oregano and sea salt, and eat while warm, or serve them atop a simple tomato salsa for a more formal presentation.

Ewe Milk Yogurt with Lilac
Elizabeth M. Street

This yogurt is a perfect backdrop for lilac's bright and subtly citrusy flavor, delicate in contrast to its famously heady perfume. Enjoy it with a drizzle of chestnut honey or stir it into a simple Persian cucumber soup. It makes a lovely sauce for roast meat or vegetables when mixed with a pinch of salt and some grassy extra-virgin olive oil.

A note about substitutions: Cow or goat milk can also be used for this recipe, but plant-based milks require a different preparation to make yogurt. Regardless of milk type, do not use ultra-pasteurized milk, as it is too sterile to culture the bacteria necessary for yogurt. Some prefer to use a mesophilic (moderate temperature–loving) culture, which will preserve the probiotic benefits of raw milk and produce a runnier, more drinkable texture. To use a mesophilic culture, do not heat the milk, but allow it to culture at room temperature until the desired tang and texture are reached.

handful of lilac blossoms, roughly ¾ cup
1 quart raw or pasteurized ewe milk
thermophilic yogurt culture or 3 tbsp
   plain store-bought yogurt

Place the lilac blossoms in a large glass or ceramic bowl. In a heavy-bottomed pot, heat the milk over medium-low heat until it looks like it's about to boil over (at least 185°F if using a thermometer), then immediately decant the milk into the bowl with the lilac blossoms. Let the mixture steep until you can just hold your little finger in the milk no more than three seconds (110–115°F); this can take about an hour depending on the temperature of the room.

Discard the lilac blossoms and, in a separate bowl, mix the thermophilic culture (following manufacturer's instructed proportions) or store-bought yogurt into 1 cup of the lilac-infused milk. Add this mixture back to the large bowl and stir well. Cover the bowl with a pot lid (it doesn't have to fit perfectly), swaddle like a newborn babe with a thick towel or blanket, then place in a spot free of drafts or cold. (I use my oven with the oven light on for warmth. Don't forget to tell your roommate not to turn on the oven!) Let the yogurt culture 9–18 hours, depending on the ambient temperature and the tartness and thickness you prefer. Refrigerate for a few hours and, if desired, strain in a colander lined with cheesecloth to thicken, reserving the whey for another use.

Rose Jelly

Asparagus with Weeds and Flowers

Rose Jelly
Lisa Li

4 tsp agar powder
3 tsp sugar
1 The Qi Shangri-la rose
brown sugar syrup or maple syrup,
  to serve

In a small bowl, combine the agar and sugar. Add 2 cups of water to a small saucepan, then add the agar mixture and stir. Bring to a boil over high heat, then reduce heat to low and cook for 2 minutes. Meanwhile, fill a large bowl with ice and cold water. Place the saucepan in the ice bath, and chill for 3 minutes, stirring occasionally.

Steep the rose in hot water for 3 minutes. Gently lift the rose from the water with a bamboo tong and place it in a high-walled round tray or mold. Pour the agar-sugar mixture over the rose and chill for 15 minutes, until the jelly has set.

Remove the rose jelly from the tray or mold, and pour the brown sugar syrup over it. Enjoy!

Edible Flowers

Marigold Bread Pudding
Eden Batki

6 slices fresh or stale white, egg, or whole
    wheat bread, torn into small pieces
1 cup whole milk or alternative milk of
    choice
½ tsp vanilla extract or 1 vanilla bean,
    scraped
½ cup brown sugar
2 tbsp fresh marigold petals, finely
    chopped
pinch of salt
2 eggs, lightly beaten
butter

Preheat oven to 350°F. Grease a loaf
pan and fill it with the pieces of bread.

Heat the milk in a pot with the vanilla,
sugar, marigold petals, and salt until warm,
then remove from heat. Whisk in the eggs
and pour the milk mixture over the bread
in the pan.

Bake for about 40 minutes, until the
top is crispy and a knife inserted into the
middle of the pudding comes out clean.
Eat warm or at room temperature.

Asparagus with Weeds and Flowers
Leif Hedendal

The impact of this recipe comes from
the wildflowers scattered at the end. I
used sweet alyssum, forget-me-nots,
black locust tree blossoms, and calendula petals, and the greens of bur chervil,
miner's lettuce, and chickweed, but any
number of different flowers and flowering
weeds would work well.

Select a handful of asparagus spears
of similar thickness, snap off the woody
ends, and partially peel the bottom
halves. Peel and trim a few baby artichokes. Bring a pot of salted water to
a boil. Parboil the artichokes for a few
minutes until not quite fully cooked.
Remove the artichokes and let drain.
Next, place the asparagus in the boiling
water and cook until tender, 2–5 minutes
depending on the thickness of the spears.

In a frying pan, place a knob of butter
and the artichokes and cook over medium heat. Sauté, moving frequently, until
the artichokes and the butter are golden
brown, then remove from heat.

To plate, arrange the vegetables
artfully. Add some fresh chèvre, extra-
virgin olive oil, a squeeze of fresh lemon,
and a little coarse salt. Finally, scatter
the plate with wildflowers.

Flower Pasta
Santiago Perez

Making pasta with edible flowers is a fun and beautiful way to prepare pasta at home. To make the dough, I recommend using 50 percent semola flour as it will help the pasta to get to a better al dente point when cooked. For every 100 g of dry ingredients (50 g semola and 50 g wheat flour combined), you will need 1 egg, 10 g of salt, and 1 tablespoon of olive oil.

To prepare the dough, make a bowl with the flour on a flat surface, and into the middle of the bowl add the eggs, salt, and oil. With your hands, working from the inside out, mix all together into a shaggy dough. Knead the dough for about 10 minutes, until it becomes uniform and smooth. Cover the dough and let it rest for at least 1 hour.

Once the dough has relaxed, divide it in two. Using a pasta maker, roll and stretch each ball of dough until you have two equally sized, 2 mm–thick rectangles. Gather the flowers and fresh herbs you would like to add to the pasta. Choose flowers that don't contain a lot of water or use only the petals to prevent the pasta from breaking when stretched. Place the flowers, petals, and fresh herbs onto one of the rectangles of dough. Place the other rectangle of dough on top and press with your fingers to join them. Pass the dough through the pasta maker again until you reach your preferred thickness.

You can cut the pasta into whatever shape you like. I like making pappardelle and serving it with butter, lemon, garlic, and sage.

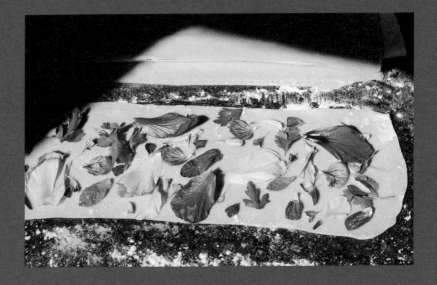

Edible Flowers

Cooking with Flowers

Thyme

Edible Flowers

Fennel Pies
(*Marathopites*)
Adrianna Glaviano

This recipe comes from the island of Crete, where wild fennel grows rampant. There are many ways of making *mara-thopites*; this is just one. The classic recipe calls for the tender leaves of the wild fennel, but all parts of the plant are edible, including its yellow flowers, which are added here. If you can't find wild fennel, you can add the soft green tops of fennel stalks.

1 ½ cups all-purpose flour
1 ½ cups whole wheat flour
1 cup water, room temperature
7 tbsp olive oil, plus more for frying
1 tbsp red or white wine vinegar
1 tsp flaky sea salt
½ cup scallions, finely chopped
2 cups wild fennel greens and flowers,
    finely chopped, plus extra for garnish
½ cup cilantro, finely chopped
1 cup greens such as wild spinach,
    dandelion greens, or mustard greens,
    finely chopped
zest of a lemon

To make the dough, in a large bowl whisk the flours together until well combined. Add the water, 5 tablespoons olive oil, vinegar, and salt and stir until a dough forms. Knead for about 5 minutes until the dough can be made into a smooth ball.

To make the filling, heat 2 tablespoons of oil in a pan over low heat and cook the scallions until just soft. Add the fennel, cilantro, greens, and lemon zest and sauté for about 5 minutes until everything becomes soft.

Make the pies by taking about ¾ cup of dough, forming two balls, and, on a floured work surface, rolling them out into small round disks. Scoop 1 tablespoon of filling onto the center of one disk and spread it evenly, leaving a little space around the edges. Then, with your finger, wet the edges with water and place the second disk of dough on top. Using a fork, crimp the edges of the disks to seal the pie. Repeat until you've made about five pies.

In a frying pan, heat about ¾ cup olive oil over medium-high heat and fry the pies on each side until they are golden brown. Sprinkle with flaky salt and scatter with fennel flowers and greens.

Cooking with Flowers

Nasturtium Pesto

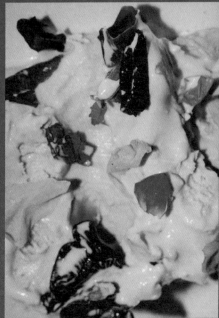

Flower Petal–Swirled Ice Cream

Nasturtium Pesto

This recipe can be made with either a mortar and pestle or a food processor. It's a loose, flexible recipe and very much about adding as you go and balancing ingredients to your taste and preferred consistency. So feel free to omit the garlic, to substitute almonds for walnuts, or to use raw or toasted nuts. The nasturtium flowers will give an orange color to the pesto, so include as many flowers as you like.

1 ½ cups nasturtium leaves
1 cup nasturtium flowers
2–3 cloves garlic
handful of walnuts
¼ cup Parmesan, grated
extra-virgin olive oil
salt and pepper to taste

Roughly chop the nasturtium leaves and flowers, garlic, and nuts and combine them with the Parmesan in a food processor or with a mortar and pestle. Slowly drizzle the olive oil into the mixture and pulse or pound until you reach your preferred consistency. Season to taste, adding salt and pepper in small pinches along the way, as the nasturtium is peppery and the Parmesan salty.

Serve with any pasta, especially with fresh pasta.

Edible Flowers

Flower Petal–Swirled
Ice Cream
Loria Stern

I was always fascinated with the sexiness of a swirl, that thread of color weaving across the vanilla canvas in a fresh scoop of ice cream. I experimented with various ways to create this sensual effect with botanicals. After freezing flower petals and noticing they take on a completely new texture (think delicate, melt-in-your-mouth), I was elated to test out my own take on the swirl. This ice cream base is my go-to, as everything is balanced, from the creaminess to the sweetness.

2 cups heavy cream
⅔ cup whole milk
⅔ cup sugar
¼ tsp kosher salt
1 tsp vanilla extract
1 tsp loose tea, dried flower petals,
    or petal dust (optional)
2 large eggs
edible flower petals of your choice

Combine the cream, milk, sugar, salt, and vanilla in a saucepan. If you are infusing the ice cream with an herb, tea, or flower, add it to the cream mixture. Bring the liquid just to a boil, stirring occasionally, and remove from the heat.

In a large bowl, lightly beat the eggs. Add the hot cream mixture to the eggs in a slow stream, whisking. Then pour the mixture back into the pan. Cook over moderately low heat, stirring constantly, until a thermometer registers 170°F. (Do not let it boil. If the custard curdles, you can blend it with a hand blender.) Pour the custard through a sieve into a clean bowl and let cool.

Chill the custard, covering the surface with plastic or a beeswax wrap (only if the custard is at room temperature) until cold, for at least 3 hours, and up to 1 day.

Freeze the custard using an ice cream maker. Then, prep your flowers. The ice cream looks lovely with petals of a variety of colors, but you don't have to use different flowers; one variety will work beautifully. Spread 3 scoops of the frozen ice cream in a container, then add a layer of flower petals (I like using scissors to cut the petals directly on top of the ice cream in order to control how large the petals are; the goal is dime-sized petals), and then repeat, alternating ice cream and flower petals. If you're using a transparent container, make sure the sides are clean so that the petals are visible.

Cover and put the container in the freezer to harden overnight. If you can't wait, you can leave it in the fridge for 4 hours and the custard will be more of a semifreddo, which is still delicious.

Tangerine Cake with Frosting and Flowers
Chula Galvez

During the 2020 coronavirus quarantine, I was in Argentina as autumn arrived. My boyfriend, who is a chef, and I spent almost every day cooking and experimenting with new recipes. One day I got a very delicious tangerine from an organic farm and decided I wanted to make a dessert in honor of that fruit. I remembered a cake I once ate that was made with orange and almond flour. I thought I could make it with cashew nut flour—I love cashews—and tangerines. And it worked so well! But something was missing to make it a proper cake: frosting and flowers. This cake is best served one day after baking.

3–4 medium tangerines
200 g cashew flour (or almond flour)
1 tsp baking powder
5 eggs
180 g sugar
100 ml heavy cream
100 g white chocolate, chopped
200 g cream cheese

Preheat the oven to 150°C/300°F. Spray a springform pan with nonstick cooking spray and set aside.

Place the tangerines in a pot and add water to cover them. Bring the water to a boil, then reduce to low and cook the tangerines for 2 hours, or until you can insert a fork easily (add more water as necessary). Discard the remaining liquid.

Remove the seeds from the tangerines and puree the whole fruits in a food processor until smooth. Weigh out 300 g of the puree and let it cool.

Combine the cashew flour and baking powder in a small bowl. Combine eggs and sugar in a medium bowl and, using an electric mixer, beat for around 10 minutes, until the mixture doubles in volume. Fold the egg mixture into the tangerine puree in two additions, trying to lose as little air as possible. Gently fold in the cashew flour mixture.

Pour the batter into the springform pan and bake for 45 minutes or until a skewer inserted in the center of the cake comes out clean. Let the cake cool in the pan and refrigerate overnight.

To prepare the frosting, begin by making a ganache: heat the cream in a small saucepan until just beginning to simmer and pour it over the white chocolate. Let it sit for 5 minutes, and then mix with a heatproof spatula. Let the mixture chill in the fridge for at least 2 hours. Once it is cold and firm, using an electric mixer, beat the cream cheese with the ganache until you get a silky and even texture.

Remove the cake from the springform pan. Be careful when you handle the cake as it is very fluffy. Cover it with the frosting and decorate it with edible flowers. Enjoy!

Cooking with Flowers

Index, Common Name

Index, Latin Name

Edible Flowers

Flowers

Aweside Farm Polegate, UK

Eagle Street Rooftop Farm
   Brooklyn, NY

Edible Gardens LA Los Angeles, CA

Farm.One

Gannon Organics Savannah, GA

One Wild Acre Charleston, SC

Salmon Creek Farm Albion, CA

Salty Acres Whidbey Island, WA

Slow Flowers slowflowers.com

Soul Fire Farm, Petersburg, NY

Treiber Farms Peconic, NY

Union Square Greenmarket
   New York, NY

Vertu Farm Savannah, GA

Weatherlow Farms Westport, MA

Windfall Farms Montgomery, NY

Further Reading

Buchmann, Stephen. *The Reason for Flowers*. New York: Scribner, 2015.

Clifton, Claire. *Edible Flowers*. New York: McGraw-Hill, 1984.

Creasy, Rosalind. *The Edible Flower Garden*. Boston: Periplus, 1990.

Gerard, John. *The Herbal, or General History of Plants*. Mineola, NY: Calla Editions, 2015.

Gordon, Jean. *The Art of Cooking with Roses*. New York: Noonday Press, 1968.

Gramp, D. & P. *Edible Flowers and Leaves*. The Culinary Library, 2013.

Hildebrand, Caz. *Herbarium*. London: Thames & Hudson, 2019.

Kirker, Constance L. and Mary Newman. *Edible Flowers: A Global History*. London: Reaktion Books, 2016.

La Cerva, Gina Rae. *Feasting Wild: In Search of the Last Untamed Food*. Vancouver: Greystone Books, 2020.

McPhee, John. *Oranges*. New York: Farrar, Straus and Giroux, 1967.

Morse, Kitty. *Edible Flowers*. Berkeley, CA: Ten Speed Press, 1995.

Pliny. *Natural History: A Selection*. New York: Penguin Classics, 1991.

Sackville-West, Vita. *Some Flowers*. London: Pavilion, 1993.

Wall Kimmerer, Robin. *Braiding Sweetgrass*. London: Penguin, 2013.

Wilkinson Barash, Cathy. *Edible Flowers: From Garden to Palate*. Golden, CO: Fulcrum, 1993.

Woodring Smith, Leona. *The Forgotten Art of Flower Cookery*. Gretna, LA: Pelican, 1985.

Weatherlow Farms

Edible Flowers

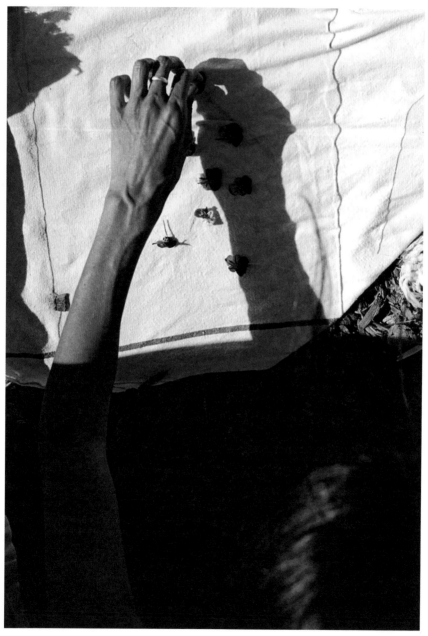

Pansies at Treiber Farms

Edible Flowers

Contributors

Eden Batki is an artist based in Los Angeles.

Christina Crawford is a chef and founder of Tart Vinegar.

Lizania Cruz is a Dominican artist.

Alexandra Cunningham Cameron is a curator of contemporary design.

Clarisse Demory is a creative director based in Paris.

Agostina Galvez is an Argentinian director and photographer.

Chula Galvez is an Argentinian chef who focuses on edible flowers.

Laila Gohar is an artist based in New York who uses food as a sculptural medium.

Leif Hedendal is an artist and chef based in California.

Hermione Hoby is a British novelist and cultural critic.

Krysta Jabczenski is a photographer based in Santa Fe.

Romano Japitana is a food writer based in Antipolo, Philippines.

Isabella Killoran is an artist and photographer.

Evangelia Koutsovoulou is the founder of Daphnis and Chloe.

Gina Rae La Cerva is an environmental anthropologist and author of *Feasting Wild*.

Lisa Li is the founder of The Qi.

Daniel McMahon is an American photographer.

Sneha Mehta is a writer and designer based in Mumbai.

Anna Morton is the founder of Leaves and Flowers.

Andi Murphy is a Navajo food journalist and host of the podcast *Toasted Sister*.

Santiago Perez is an Argentinian chef.

Claire Ratinon is an organic food grower and writer based in England.

Aurora Robles is a designer based in Los Angeles.

Julia Sherman is an artist and author of *Salad for President*.

Fanny Singer is an art writer and author of *Always Home*.

Loria Stern is a baker who uses edible flowers extensively.

Elizabeth M. Street is a cook based in Richmond, Virginia.

Heidi Swanson is a chef and cookbook author.

Tara Thomas is a vegan chef and activist based in New York.

Sri Venudas is a yoga teacher from Kerala, India.

Thank You

To compile a book like this, one needs an active community to tap into, an energy that is already burgeoning. With a topic like edible flowers, there is a bounty. My acknowledgments first and foremost are to everyone eating, foraging, filming, photographing, experimenting with, trespassing to collect, and reclaiming these blossoms. Thank you, of course, to my editor at Monacelli, Jenny Florence, and to Adrianna Glaviano, both of whom responded YES when I first mentioned this idea, and who, to the very end, have been the most ardent collaborators. Adrianna and I wanted to make something that felt hyphenate: historical-readable-beautiful-immersive, with flowers that are not photographed "cheesy" and with text that gives just enough to rouse your curiosity—to perhaps see beyond the ornamental and bring the natural world a bit closer.

Our first drive was to Treiber Farms where Pete Treiber generously let us collect and photograph our first twenty flowers. The rest were sourced and found with thanks to Windfall Farms, Phoebe Poole at Weatherlow Farms, Longwood Gardens, Orto Botanico dell'Università di Roma "La Sapienza," the SCAD community garden, a hollyhock that fell in someone's yard in Brooklyn Heights, and wildflowers on the sides of many roads.

Thank you to all of the contributors, who introduced us to new flowers, and added an imperative layer to the content of this book. Thank you to Lisa Forbes for letting us cover your apartment with flowers and for eating many floral meals together. Thank you to my family, and my second family, the Streets. And thank you (from both Adrianna and me) in no specific order to Anouck Bertin, Alex Brack, Dan McMahon, Isabella Killoran, Claire Hungerford, Yasmeen Khaja, and all of our friends who answered calls for searches for very specific flowers. Thank you to Sneha Mehta, who jumped in at the perfect moment. And to Molly Marquand, whose botanical knowledge is unmatched. Lastly, thank you to everyone reading this book. I hope that it inspires the impulse to eat, live with, and think about flowers.

Treiber Farms

The flowers referred to in this book are generally acknowledged to be safe, but neither the author nor the publisher can be held responsible for any adverse reaction which any particular individual experiences. Consuming edible flowers in large quantities, flowers that have been misidentified, flowers that have been treated with pesticides, or inedible parts of the plant may cause harmful effects. The author of this book is neither a horticulturist nor a professional forager. It is the responsibility of the reader to exercise their best judgement and secure flowers from a knowledgeable source.

Library of Congress Control Number: 2021940151

ISBN 978-1-58093-571-5

Printed in China

Monacelli
A Phaidon Company
65 Bleecker Street
New York, NY 10012
www.monacellipress.com

All photographs by Adrianna Glaviano unless otherwise noted:

Clarisse Demory 30
Romano Japitana 34
Dan McMahon 70, 78, 79
Isabella Killoran 101
Krysta Jabczenski 135
Agostino Galvez 232, 244, 251
Aurora Robles 240
Monica Nelson 241
Lisa Li 242 (left)
Leif Hedendal 242 (right)